I dedicate this book
to Jim and Janette
and the whole Schueller family
who taught us all what
Commitment to Change means

First Edition

Edited by Jeff Hufnagel

Commitment to Change

The 5 Cs that Transform Your Life and Business

by Greg Olney

Forward by Jeff Hufnagel

Acknowledgements

My son Nathan for getting me through the hard times and loving me through my mistakes; my daughter Danielle for being daddy's girl; Thomas Johnston for helping me understand quiet leadership; my Mother & Dad for always being there; my brother Glen for being my friend and true brother; my sister Kim for being the strong woman that she is; The entire Olney family; Cassy Schepperle for her commitments; Marie Austin for her love of family; David Schepperle for being my friend and someone I can count on; The entire Schepperle family; Michelle Olney for over 20 years of lessons and a lot of happiness mixed in; Jim, Janette, Sierra, Skylar, and Slater Schueller and the whole Schueller family for showing us the way to succeed; Denise & Scott Weisheit for being my counselors and best friends; Melanie & Sean Oliver for being my business coach, friends, and wise counsel; Solomon Cheifer for being my legal counsel, my wise counsel, and friend; Ernie, Kim and the Hinojosa family for helping me write the workbook; Mark & Jenny Loomis for being there; Dan Loomis for being my friend; Mike & Velma Hannah for staying with me while my hair started to grow again; Duane Roquemore and family for their heart for God; Mike Stefano for fixing my Achilles and relationships; Pat Roy for our pact; Melanie & Jay Blakeborough for their prayers; The Greene family for their insight; Al Acuna and his family for sticking by; Myriam & David Bourbinay for their heart; Seth Schmidt for keeping me focused; Ken Campbell for reminding me where home is; Linda Carlberg of BrandLand Marketing for bringing this book together; Jeff Hufnagel for his awesome editing abilities; Roger Richardson for helping me with the Theory of Constraints; Seta & Peter Stephan for their friendship and integrity; Garen Stephan for showing me what coaching is; Cecil Purchase for his business sense; Joe Lawson for coming alongside me and being a great friend; Joe and Linda Castro for their friendship; J Moyer for being my friend, wanting me to succeed, and providing me a way to do it; Tim Lietaert for making me part of his family and giving me an outlet; Brian Boyd for being my financial guy, my wise counsel, and friend; Steve Wack for his wise counsel, strength, and being a great friend; Mark Rasche for his head for business, life, and God; Susie Vinokur, Johnson Ahn, and Tammi Hartman for staying in touch; Darryl Wooldridge for his stability; Nena Dols for her wise counsel; and most importantly, Almighty God.

Table Of Contents

The First C: Consideration

The Second C: Certainty

The Third C: Charter

The Fourth C: Character

The Fifth C: Commitment

Table of Contents

Preface

I'm writing this book to fulfill my purpose to affect change in others so that they can do great things. I purposely used the word 'affect' in my purpose statement because that word, 'affect', describes an act upon something instead of 'effect', which is something that is produced by that act. I may have no idea what change is being accomplished by the many that will read this book, *Commitment to Change*, and my last book, *The Transition Game*. It's more important to me that the message has been communicated so that an accomplishment can be obtainable by each reader. I care about the *Commitment to Change* that comes about in each person as they understand the concepts in these two books. It's important to me that great change (in quality rather than actual size of change) happens in each person's life, but I've relegated myself to the fact that I won't know what has happened in others' lives while I achieve my purpose. It's less important to me that I know about it rather than it happened in the first place.

I've written these books because I've learned how to reverse-engineer my attitudes and behaviors. Simply, I've taken my attitudes and behaviors apart piece by piece so that I can understand how they work. I've reasoned out the decision-making process through years of research and shoveled out my legacy-thinking to replace the incorrect and incomplete construction of myself so that I can function as I was originally designed. This process is far from complete. But I will finish my life better than I began because I fought this good fight.

The way that each of us can fight this fight is to commit to it. We must:

- **"Contemplate"** our attitudes and behaviors so that we can each reverse-engineer them piece by piece.
- Take an **"oath"** to change for the better by learning how to begin, transition, and make a great *Commitment to Change*.
- Not do this alone. We need others. We need our close circle of advisors with whom we can have a **"meeting of the minds"** and receive good counsel.
- Change our make-up. That means we must get in touch with the **"moral fiber"** that is in each of us. That will lead us to successful change in the right way.

- **"Initiate"** the successful change in the right way. The shelf life of unrealized change is short. No successful change ever happened that wasn't started.
- Go through a **"transformation"** by renewing our minds so that we can find what is good, acceptable, and perfect.

This process spells **COMMIT** and that is how we will win *The Transition Game*.

Contemplate
Oath
Meeting of the minds
Moral fiber
Initiate
Transformation

Foreword

I have learned to embrace change and I can honestly tell you that the commitment to do so did not always come easily or naturally.

One thing I know to be certain at this stage in my life, is that regular change can and will occur throughout life. It will occur regularly in your job and in your personal life. The challenge is whether or not we actually recognize, initiate, and commit to these opportunities for successful change and whether there is a realization that they provide true opportunities of growth and internal satisfaction for each of us.

Most of our adult professional lives are spent working inside and outside of organizations with diverse personalities. We go about our days watching how individuals work and interact with others. We weigh our strengths and weaknesses against others we associate with, and we go about executing our daily job requirements. Our private lives are quite often a microcosm of our professional lives and are also rich in challenges, tasks, relationships, and commitments. Change is a critical part of our lives there as well. Our daily lives are a series of potential changes. Practically anyone working or living in today's competitive and fast-paced world can relate to this.

What is interesting is just how much paralysis and hand-wringing there is associated with the word "change." So many people shy away from change and paint it in such a negative light. They don't understand that successful change cannot be realized if it is never started. You don't believe me? Just try mentioning change at your place of work and watch how many of your fellow employees will go running back to their desks dreading the next potential company transformation or transition. It's practically the same reaction that occurs when your favorite restaurant changes their menu, your favorite sports team changes their uniforms, or your neighborhood grocery store changes the layout of the store. People love familiarity and resist change. It's just a fact of life (even if it's positive change).

Very few individuals invest the time, energy, and determination necessary to understand just how enriching a strong commitment to successful change can be. I'm not entirely sure this is due to a lack of initiative. Rather there are just not a lot of good roadmaps that exist today to help us understand how to embrace and commit to making a change. That is why it is necessary that we all are exposed to someone or a method that can simplify, decode, and/or reconstruct this often confusing process for us, so that we can all benefit from our own personal commitment to change.

Several months ago, I was attending an all-day seminar hosted by an executive coaching organization. One of the members asked if anyone could recommend a book that would assist her in becoming more comfortable with the journey her life was taking. She was going through a separation and a job transition. I recommended she read Greg Olney's book, *The Transition Game*. She asked how Greg's book would help. I told her that if anyone understood change dynamics and what it took to initiate successful/meaningful change better than Greg, I would be very surprised.

In Greg's book, *The Transition Game*, he describes how to navigate between status quo and an actual commitment to change. I saw Greg's ability first hand as he worked as a consultant within our organization with a goal of increasing our group's comfort with change and demonstrated how to make real meaningful changes. He helped in removing the negativity associated with change and transformed the organization's attitude toward change so that we were executing through transition stages and then initiating and embracing actual change. Over time, our group made a commitment to refuse to linger in the status quo that was affecting our company's results and progress. With Greg's help we reconstructed our past behaviors and indecisiveness and began our transformation into a company that valued and initiated successful change.

In his new book, *Commitment to Change*, Greg elaborates in much more detail the final stage of *The Transition Game*. He expands on the five pieces that make up a strong and lasting Commitment to Change by discussing key elements such as Consideration, Certainty, Charter, Character, and Commitment.

I wholeheartedly recommend that you read this book. From individuals to family members to leaders of large organizations, we all need to learn how to better embrace and commit to initiating successful change in order to be able to reach our personal and strategic goals and objectives.

I have learned to embrace change and I can honestly tell you that the commitment to do so did not always come easily or naturally. However, after reading Greg's books, I see change as a far more meaningful process and no longer dread or delay the commitment to change.

Jeff Hufnagel, 2013
Chief Operating Officer
CBM Services, Inc.

Introduction

The "5 Cs" noted in the subtitle go beyond that. What we'll explore together in this book is that commitment is only the final piece in the whole *Transition Game* model. That's how we will find 5 pieces. Those pieces include: Consideration, Certainty, Charter, Character, and finally Commitment. Each 'C' is essential to a strong and vibrant *Commitment to Change*.

- **Consideration** comes when we evaluate the facts and give careful thought before deliberately charging forward. This first step is when we do our risk assessment and cost/benefit analysis. We must consider if our *Commitment to Change* is right before moving to the next step.

- **Certainty** arises once we've evaluated the facts and are fully convinced that your *Commitment to Change* is right. We can be confident that this commitment leaves no doubt in each person's mind that it is each person's way to fulfill their purpose.

- **Charter** is an outline of conditions for each *Commitment to Change*. A charter organizes and defines who does what by when. It can similarly be thought of as the contract to get things done.

- **Character** encompasses the qualities of a person's life. It is the accumulation of all of a person's features and attributes that form the individual nature of a person. Character includes elements like honesty, courage, integrity, trustworthiness, and care for others that build someone's reputation.

- **Commitment** is the final stage of *The Transition Game*. Once we've gotten over the *Status Quo* and the *Fear* of moving forward, we *Balance* and begin *Doing What it Takes* to reach our *Commitment to Change*. Commitment is the overriding theme of *The Transition Game* where *Consideration* brings *Certainty* and guidance from the *Charter* brings *Character*.

This book is spread out over these 5 Cs so that we can delve into each section and understand these sections piece by piece. I challenge you to read this book and learn this process so you can reach your own *Commitment to Change*.

Commitment to Change

The 5 Cs that Transform Your Life and Business

by Greg Olney

Forward by Jeff Hufnagel

THE FIRST C:
Consideration

Chapter 1
Empty Slots

Empty Slots

My dad worked in other countries, had top-secret security clearance from the United States government, and functioned alongside other foreign governments. He was an expert in negotiation and decision making. One of the comments that he always made was that decisions are made based on empty slots of information. If you think about it, you wouldn't need to make a decision at all for a Commitment to Change if the Status Quo is good enough. If the Status Quo was good enough, then information is complete.

If faced with an option between certain death and paradise, there is no doubt about the right option. There is no judgment call when a mind doesn't need to be made up. Then there would be no empty slots of information. That's why you'll see the strongest Commitment to Change with someone who has their mind made up and is laser-focused.

A focused person is so sure of their destination that they have sold out for it. They will run the race, accomplish the task, and nothing will stop them. I'm sure you've heard stories of a knight protecting his princess or a Secret Service agent protecting the President. They are focused individuals that don't have empty slots of information that will cause a judgment call to occur telling them that what they're doing may or may not be right. They already know the destination. They've researched the empty slots. These people will fight to the death for what they believe in.

Critical Mass

There's a lot to be said for momentum, but thinking that momentum is enough for long-lasting change is a self-defeating concept. Momentum is not important until it becomes sufficient enough in a family, business, or sports setting where it becomes self-sustaining and produces further growth. That is critical mass.

Critical Mass can also happen in a riot situation where mob-mentality rules and people lose self-control. Momentum is still important in this situation, but it acts negatively. Momentum in this situation becomes self-sustaining and the riot feeds on itself. We've seen it time and time again when a mob loses control and acts like an out of control fire.

In business, a critical mass point is the stage when the value gained is greater than the price paid. As long as the price is set above the targeted cost, a profit is realized and the business stays viable. Critical Mass won't last forever though. Usually, a saturation point is reached without some outside force acting on the business to sustain profitability.

We see Critical Mass happening when it makes sense for a supermarket to be built. It may take a few thousand families to support one supermarket. There are other factors that affect this critical mass. Those factors may include the location of the supermarket, the size of the market, and the public opinion or stigma for or against the market. Small changes in these factors may swing Critical Mass wildly.

See what fits into your business or family mission statement and figure out what it takes to attain Critical Mass with the ventures that will cause a self-sustaining chain reaction that will continue.

Theory of Constraints

Essentially, our output is based on the capacity of our constraints. It's as simple as that. A team is only as strong as its weakest player. A chain is only as strong as its weakest link. I could stop there with this explanation and that would be enough, but I want to provide an example in these following steps so that we can learn how to be productive in our relationships and in business. Dr. Eli Goldratt originally described the steps listed below as a process that we must go through to expand constraints so that productivity is not limited in our business or our personal lives. In order to expand constraints, we must:

1. Identify the constraint
2. Exploit the constraint
3. Focus on the constraint

4. Elevate the constraint

5. Return to step 1 as many times as is necessary

I would like to say that this section of my book was my creation, but it actually came from a discussion with a manager who reported to me when I was with Automatic Data Processing (ADP). The manager's name was Roger Richardson. Roger is also a friend and he used the Theory of Constraints to build a strong team in the Technical Services division of Shared Services at ADP. He started with himself though.

Roger came to me after we had started the turn-around of our Technical Services team from being dead last in the country with respect to almost every performance measurement to finishing at the top instead. When he showed up in my office, he had identified himself as a potential constraint. He was resigning his position because he needed to move out of state for family reasons. Even though he was a key contributor with a revamped team and much success, he realized that having someone spearhead a team from a different state would be difficult for the staff as a whole. However, I knew that it could be done with the right leader. We could exploit the constraint. Roger had already built enough relational equity with his staff so that they would be accepting of this move. We also didn't need to utilize any additional technical connectivity that would have been expensive to change. Roger used his technical background so that no additional costs were incurred and there was not a reason for upgrades. He was able to focus on the constraint to ensure that his move appeared seamless to clients and to his staff. The constraint was elevated. Sure…there were times that Roger needed to tweak his systems so that the process would work. As such, he did spend extra time on the phone with his staff, but ultimately, the transition was well-received and handled nicely. After Roger's move, we continued to be #1 and #2 in almost every performance measurement across the country.

The difference with optimization and the Theory Of Constraints (TOC) is that with optimization, each constraint is viewed as a limiting factor to the scope of services. With TOC, however, Roger used the constraint as a focusing instrument to broaden the process. He was able to move to a different state and accomplish both his work and family goals by gaining agreement on the problem in the first place. He was able to then direct and solve the problem by eliminating potential negative impact and implementing a solution despite any obstacles.

Pick One or Two Goals and Kick the Crap Out of Them

Pick One or Two Things and Kick the Crap Out of Them

Josh Weston was probably one of the best CEOs that I have ever encountered. His mindset was that we would pick one or two projects, ventures, or goals and kick the crap out of them. This catapulted Automatic Data Processing into a company worth billions of dollars. I did eventually clean this saying up substantially, but the translation remains: Don't try the scatter-gun approach on your goals.

A goal is merely a desired result. You can expand on a goal by setting an expectation that the process to get to the goal will develop in some order or by placing a deadline by which that goal will be obtained. However, the goal itself is just the desired result. When we have too many goals, our desk becomes cluttered and we are easily distracted. My business coach, Sean Oliver, put me through a goal exercise, which helped me prioritize my goals and become more like Josh Weston.

This Excel spreadsheet (shown on the previous page) can be found free on my website, www.gonatelle.com. When my life becomes overly cluttered and I find my Commitment to Change becoming my commitment to multiple changes, I use this spreadsheet to understand what's really important at the time. If you have a lot of goals facing you and you want to focus on one or two, start plugging in all of your goals to the worksheet. If you have less than 16 goals at the beginning, that's good. Fill in every other cell and then go back to the top and fill in the blank spaces.

I strongly suggest having a "loser's bracket" because if you're picking more than one goal and you're prioritizing, your #1 goal will win out against all comers. Your # 2 goal may lose out early to your #1 goal and you may miss an important objective in your life or business.

I've used this and have been amazed at the success. I welcome you to join me and do the same.

Lessons Learned

To start the *Commitment to Change*, which is the fifth and final step of *The Transition Game*, we need to go through a stage of consideration. We must make decisions that are based on empty slots of information. If the *Status Quo* is good enough, then information is complete and no new

Commitment to Change is necessary. There is no judgment call when a mind doesn't need to be made up because there are no empty slots of information. The strongest *Commitment to Change* happens with sharp focus. It helps to know the destination by researching empty slots of information.

It helps, though, to have concrete goals. A goal is just a desired result. If you have too many desires, you will become distracted. Please revisit the spreadsheet in this chapter that puts your goals in competition so that you can find your top one or two goals that will win out. Use this spreadsheet to understand what's really important and utilize a "loser's bracket" to find your #2 goal.

Momentum is not enough for long-lasting change. Momentum is not important until it becomes sufficient enough in a family, business, or sports setting where it becomes self-sustaining and produces further growth. That is Critical Mass. Critical mass in business is the stage when the value gained is greater than the price paid. Small changes in Critical Mass factors may swing critical mass wildly. It's important to stay ahead of the curve, figure out what it takes to attain critical mass, and understand what will cause a self-sustaining chain reaction that will continue.

Our output is based on the capacity of our constraints. A chain is only as strong as its weakest link. In order to expand constraints, we must identify, exploit, focus on, and then elevate the constraint so that we can increase our productivity. The difference with optimization and the Theory Of Constraints (TOC) is that with optimization, each constraint is viewed as a limiting factor to the scope of services. With TOC, however, constraints are used as a focusing instrument to broaden the process. We can solve problems by eliminating potential negative impact and implementing a solution despite any obstacles.

Chapter 2
Necessary & Sufficient

Necessary & Sufficient

There are two kinds of conditions that will drive you to your *Commitment to Change*: Necessary conditions and sufficient conditions. What is necessary may not be sufficient. A necessary condition is a circumstance that restricts, modifies, or limits *Commitment to Change*. If I say that a particular *Commitment to Change* can only exist under certain conditions, then those certain conditions are necessary. As an example, my car will only run if I put gas in it. If I don't have gas in my car, my car won't run. In this situation, gas is a necessary condition for my car to run.

Married couples may go through necessary and sufficient conditions. One or both of them may be doing what's necessary. Staying in the relationship is necessary to keep the marriage alive. But even though staying in a situation may be necessary, it may not be sufficient to keep the marriage alive. If you know that the right thing to do is to keep your marriage alive, then you will do what is also sufficient, which is to love and respect each other without becoming intolerant towards the other person.

Often, one spouse may not do what is necessary because the other spouse is not doing what is sufficient to sustain the relationship. This is apparent when one spouse leaves the household because the other spouse is not showing love or respect. You may also notice couples doing only what is necessary and not doing what is sufficient when a spouse just stays in the *Status Quo* because they know it's the only way to keep the marriage alive. However, they may be harboring ill-will towards the other spouse. As such, not showing love or respect.

In order for a marriage to be alive and vibrant, both partners must do what is necessary AND sufficient. If the marriage goes south, it is the partner's fault that didn't do what was necessary and it's the partner's fault that didn't do what was sufficient. Of course, marriage is not all that important to a lot of people. We all hear of celebrities getting married one month and getting divorced the next. When we become desensitized to marriage and it becomes a byword, then it may not be all that important to do what's necessary OR what's sufficient.

Doing what's necessary happens in business when the necessary condition must be satisfied for a company's Mission Statement to be fulfilled. If you remember in my last book, "The Transition Game," the Mission Statement is simply what it takes to get to where your organization is going. The sufficient condition is fulfilled when you get to where your organization is going. The company's Vision Statement declares where your organization is going in advance. When there is a sufficient condition, the fulfillment of the Vision Statement is assured.

There was a situation that turned ugly with two people that reported to me and I brought them in separately to talk with them. From an outsider's perspective, one person plainly did nothing wrong. Regardless, I sat down with that person and, as I expected, the first question that came up was, "why are you talking to me? You can plainly see [the other person] was wrong." I then explained that the individual didn't know how I was addressing the situation with the other person and he would probably never know because that was a confidential matter, but I was there to talk to him and the focus for our conversation was to be the part that he played. I went on to say that even if one party is 99% wrong and the party to whom I was speaking was only 1% wrong, I needed to address that 1%. This person wound up giving all 100%. He did what was sufficient because he took counsel and worked on that 1%. I respect this man in his business and family life.

How many people in business commit to doing only what's necessary by just clocking in and out each day? They do the bare minimum and squeak by. Those people turn into drones that mindlessly work just to get through the day. People that don't do what's necessary usually weed themselves out because there are requirements on a job that must be fulfilled. Unless there is some distorted contract, you won't keep your job if you don't meet the minimum requirements,. People that do not do what is sufficient in business are harder to handle. They may know what it takes to make a business successful, but they don't put in that whole 100%. The only way to turn a company into a company that fully realizes their *Commitment to Change* is to have people that will do what is necessary AND sufficient. If this necessary and sufficient condition is instilled in the management team and the people with that culture are attracted and retained, your company will win.

What Are You Looking to Communicate?

What are you looking to communicate with your *Commitment to Change*? Everyone wants to communicate something. When my daughter was a teenager, she said she wanted a belly button ring. I knew she was not a fan of pain so this was a half-hearted gesture and she was really just seeking my opinion. I simply asked her, "What are you hoping to communicate with a belly button ring?" She was instantly frustrated with the answer and accused me of trying to "Dr. Phil" her. I said, "I'm not trying to 'Dr. Phil' you, I was just interested in what you were trying to communicate with a belly button ring." Everyone communicates something with what they say and do. If I walk down the street in a certain manner, I am communicating something. Regardless of anyone listening, the encoding piece of the communication puzzle is in place. When my daughter talked to me about a belly button ring, she wasn't prepared to think about what she was communicating with that belly button ring. Secretly, and she may not admit this, I believe she never wanted one in the first place because she didn't necessarily connect with what the belly button ring communicated and she's not a fan of pain. What my question allowed her to do was to get away from any peer pressure that might have been forcing her to do it in the first place. It's a lot easier to say, "My dad won't let me get a belly button ring" rather than "I don't want a belly button ring." If friends or family guide you in a direction you don't want to go, it's easier to say, "I can't" rather than "I won't."

Saying "I won't" communicates choice and leadership. Saying "I can't" communicates dependency and weakness. Which are you looking to communicate? Be prepared with an answer because everyone will be covertly or overtly challenged when they make an "I won't" statement. Rebuttals to the "I won't" statement normally start with a "Why won't you?" question, which after you've answered has one of the following tag-along trap questions.

Be careful of these tag-along trap questions. They are commonly used by salespeople to induce someone to say "yes":

- [Change your answer slightly] That's your real question, isn't it?
- That's the very reason you should buy, wouldn't you agree?
- Is that the only reason?
- If the reasons were eliminated, then would you buy?
- Could you make a decision today if you liked the proposal?
- Why? (Asking "Why?" 4 more times)
- How would what I'm offering benefit you?
- Are you with me so far?
- Getting you to say "yes" to any unrelated question so you get accustomed to the word "yes."

Be careful of this last point because there are occasions when you should answer, "Yes." Don't feel pressured to always say, "No" either. There are plainly questions when you should answer "Yes" and there are plainly questions when you should answer "No." The rest of your answers are a choice. Don't mix up your Yes's and No's. Let your Yes be Yes and your No be No.

Salespeople will try to induce you to change your No to a Yes, but if they don't care about you, they won't care if the yes or no will be a benefit to you. When you communicate, don't be like an uncaring salesperson. Care about the person with whom you are communicating. Communicate that you care and look for ways to communicate so that the person decoding your message feels cared for. Don't overuse techniques on people. People can ultimately tell when you don't care.

Stand for Something

Here's a thought: Stand for something you don't see!

All of our worldly goods will fade away. We've all heard the saying, "you can't take it with you when you're dead." No truer statement has been said. You never see a moving van behind a funeral procession. Instead, stand for something now and use your wealth to drive toward your commitment. Stand ready and seek your *Commitment to Change* earnestly. Stand even though nobody else will. Don't do what everyone else does. The results based on a wrong *Commitment to Change* produce nothing.

Stand by someone else and for the dignity of others and never ever let anyone or anything divide you and your loved ones. Benjamin Franklin said, "We must hang together or, surely, we shall hang separately." If one part of your family suffers, everyone in your family suffers. If one part is honored, every part is honored.

15 ways to stand

1. Stand up for each other
2. Be devoted to each other
3. Honor others above yourself
4. Share with those in need
5. Practice hospitality
6. Be kind to enemies
7. Be joyful
8. Be patient
9. Be faithful
10. Live in harmony with each other as much as it's possible and as much as it depends on you
11. Shake off pride
12. Associate with prisoners
13. Don't be conceited
14. Stand in the gap for someone else
15. Lead

We need to figure out what our roles are in life so that we can take a stand in the proper manner. I have different roles and each of these ways described is part of my role as a father, mate, son, leader, subordinate, catalyst, friend, and a Christian man. After I define each role, I must define the commitments to each role and ensure that they are not in competition with each other. Then, when my roles and commitments are aligned, I need to conduct myself in a manner worthy of my position. In this way we can all stand firm and strive together toward the goal not being frightened by those who oppose us. This is a sign to our opposition that we will prevail.

Wait! Did number 12 say that a way to stand is to associate with prisoners? Well, I can't leave this list without addressing the questions in your mind about this. If you're an ex-con who's not allowed to associate with other prisoners, then this, obviously, doesn't mean you. If you're tempted to do the same things as the prisoners do if they're doing something bad, this may not mean you either. My point here is that everyone has a natural inclination to be a prisoner of something. It could be something as harmful as drugs and alcohol or it could be something seemingly harmless like being a prisoner to your schedule. If you have fought the good fight and won over these things that have handcuffed you and made you a prisoner, then associate with those around you that struggle with the same vices and help them out of this bondage too.

If we take a disciplined stand based on these ideas, we will be productive. We will stand for order, which keeps us from being ineffective and unproductive.

Lessons Learned

Necessary conditions and sufficient conditions drive everyone to their own *Commitment to Change*, but just what's necessary may not be sufficient. A necessary condition is a circumstance that restricts, modifies, or limits *Commitment to Change*. Even though staying in a situation may be necessary to fulfill the *Commitment to Change*, it may not be sufficient to keep it alive. In order to keep a *Commitment to Change* alive and vibrant, you must do what is necessary AND sufficient. When there is a sufficient condition, a vision can be assured. How many of us have solely done what's necessary and done the bare minimum to just squeak by. We turn into mindless drones when this happens. The only way to fully realize our *Commitment to Change* is to have people that will do what is necessary AND sufficient.

Everyone wants to communicate something and everyone communicates something with what they say and do. Regardless of whether or not anyone is listening, the encoding piece of the communication puzzle is in place. Saying "I won't" communicates choice and leadership. Saying "I can't" communicates dependency and weakness. But be prepared with an answer when you say "I won't" because everyone is covertly or overtly challenged when they make an "I won't" statement. Let your "Yes" be "Yes" and your "No" be "No" and don't be induced into changing your "No" to a "Yes." When you communicate, don't be uncaring. Rather, care about the person with whom you are communicating. Communicate that care…and look for ways to communicate so that the person decoding your message feels cared for. Don't overuse techniques on people. People can ultimately tell when you don't care.

Stand for something you don't see! You can't take it with you when you're dead. Stand for something now and use your wealth to drive toward your commitment. Stand ready and seek your *Commitment to Change* earnestly…and stand even though nobody else will. Don't do what everyone else does. Also, stand by someone else and for the dignity of others and never ever let anyone or anything divide you and your loved ones. If one part suffers, every part suffers. If one part is honored, every part is honored.

We need to figure out what our roles are in life so that we can take a stand in the proper manner. After each role is defined, the commitments to each role must be defined to ensure that commitments are not in competition with each other. When roles and commitments are aligned you can then conduct yourself in a manner worthy of your position. With that being said you can stand firm and strive toward the goal not being frightened by those who oppose you. This is a sign to your opposition that you will prevail.

Chapter 3
Decisive Factors

6 Decisive Factors

The following factors should be used to decide whether your Commitment to Change is a right and worthwhile effort.

1. Bigger Bang for the Buck
2. Ease of Implementation
3. Available Resources
4. Biggest Positive Cost/Benefit Analysis
5. Fits Best with Purpose/Mission Statement
6. Best for Long-Term Success

A Bigger Bang for the Buck

The phrase "Bigger Bang for the Buck" originated in the 1950's to describe nuclear deterrents and the security they provided at less cost. Without expounding upon the origination of this term any further, we will use the phrase to describe how much value a decision provides at minimized cost.

Taking a train to work would be a good example for some people. People can leverage their free time on the train to start their workday earlier. They can bring their lap-top or have meditation time while saving money on fuel. Their dollar and time goes further and these people realize a greater value for a smaller cost. Taking a train to work may not work for everyone, but getting more for less is a good starting point when making a right decision.

Consider "automation" as another example of a bigger bang for the buck. I consider automation a cornerstone of any plan when I come into a new business to consult. Automation works in a family too. If we can reduce the amount of time we work in our family and instead work on our family, we will be in a better position. As an example, unless doing the dishes by hand is a family event that is used for relationship building, using a dishwasher will allow more time invested on relationships instead and that will yield a greater reward. In a work setting, automation improves employee output and the probability that functions will work and be accurate is much greater. Before long, you'll see other areas where processes can be reproduced and valuable time saved.

Ease of Implementation

How easy is something going to be to get off the ground? If something painful is easy to solve, the decision becomes a no-brainer. The question about what decision to make becomes a little more complicated when you're faced with multiple solutions or options to solve a problem. A lot can be said for timing. If a service or product launch can be done immediately and easily and if waiting would mean an opportunity lost, the decision may be painful, but the conclusion is apparent. We'll need to consider the impact on other projects and diverted focus when judging whether something is easy to implement. Even if a project seems easy, the challenge of diverted focus or impact on other projects may toughen the landscape.

Available Resources

An available resource is something that exists independently or is self-contained and ready to be consumed so that we can obtain a benefit from it. If the resource is limited or non-renewable, you may have to allocate and manage these resources. However, if you don't have resources available at all to you, your decision not to go down a certain path becomes easy. Think about a situation in which you are traveling a far distance, but your car's full gas tank would not get you the complete distance between gas stations. Making a decision not to go on the trip becomes much easier. If your goal is to finish the trip, you would not be able to meet your goal without an available resource.

Families work in the same way. If your goal is to have a family that is united and can function as useful members of society and will produce children who generate their own valuable families, you must have available resources to get you to that goal. If your family does not have the capacity to love each other, but someone in the family has a goal for a functioning and united family, counseling may be an option. Consuming this available resource will teach a family how to be united and functional and it can give them the capacity to love.

The best kind of resource is a renewable resource. My friend Pat Roy and I made a pact to raise strong 30-year olds. What we meant was that we would guide our children practically, emotionally, and spiritually when they were young so that they would grow up to be functioning and strong adults at 30 years of age. That seems like a simple pact, but Pat and I would not have been able to meet this goal if we didn't become an available resource for our children and spouses. We also would not have become that available resource without honing the skills necessary to do the job. Now our children have become a resource for others. They are Human Capital, so to speak.

Biggest Positive Cost/Benefit

In my last book, *The Transition Game*, I wrote about cost/benefit analysis in a chapter titled Peeling Back the Onion. I spoke about understanding the trade-offs in our lives and Sir Isaac Newton's third law of motion, which says that every action has an equal and opposite reaction. For every benefit, there is a cost associated with that benefit. When doing a cost/benefit analysis, if the cost of following a certain direction is greater than the benefit (and does not positively affect another benefit), then the direction should not be taken.

As you peel back the onion, be intentional and deliberate about understanding the trade-offs, costs, and benefits. It will happen at times that a transition to a seemingly wonderful benefit may mean a cost that is greater than that benefit. Consider the risks to your finances and reputation along with the potential loss of not taking your course of action.

Fits Best with Purpose/Mission Statement

Your Transition Game starts with a purpose. A purpose is why you're here in the first place. A mission is how you'll get to your Commitment to Change. Every step of the decision-making process needs to be aligned with the purpose and mission, which will support the vision. The vision is where you're going. A transition may start with a purpose, but a Commitment to Change starts with a vision and is completed with a mission. You have to know how you will change to commit to it.

Many times when I consult with businesses, we are faced with tough decisions. These tough decisions often become a lot easier when I drive the organization back to the Purpose and Mission Statement and ask the following questions:

- Does this decision match up with how we have set out to get to our goals?
- Does this decision align with why we are here in the first place?

Asking and answering these two questions well, means that the decision you make will be solid. Much time will need to be invested with building the purpose and mission statements (after the leader has a vision of where his or her team is headed). Here's a question: "After you're dead, will people say that you lived your mission?" Think about that before you start slapping together a half-hearted mission statement. You cannot just slap something together and expect it to guide solid performance. Tweaking along the way may also be necessary to ensure these questions and resulting answers will lead to good decisions.

Best for long–term success

Dr. Edward C. Banfield, a sociologist, wrote a book in the 1970's called "The Unheavenly City"[1]. In this book Banfield described the concept of "long time perspective." According to his research, it appears that people who were the most successful were those who had this long time perspective. With every decision they made, this long time perspective came into consideration. The longer the period of time, the more likely a person would achieve greatness. Individuals with long time perspectives are willing to pay the price. It may be years before success is realized, but they are willing to keep forging ahead because their perspective tells them that there is success in the future. They perform a cost/benefit analysis and do not just regard the short-term success in their minds. These people will think decades into the future.

Granted, there is no discounting the short-term. If you are unable to make it out of the short-term, there will be no long-term. I have a major character flaw. I think long-term (or long time) so much that I may disregard the short-term. The very people with whom I plan to enjoy my long-term success are the people that may not be around when that long-term success comes. There is nothing more important in this life than relationships and the right relationships should not be destroyed so that long-term success can be realized.

I have to constantly monitor myself to view the scenery as I'm going through this life. Michelle Olney, the wife I lost, said she felt like the china when I did my impersonation of a bull in a china shop. I would wreak havoc by "bulldozing" people and things in my path in order to get to the long-term success that I desired. I started learning that I would not discount short-term success if it came between me and the people I hold dear.

Still, there is pain involved with considering long-term success as more important than what we're temporarily going through. So a balance needs to be brought between what is worth the pain in the long-term without destroying those important relationships in the short-term. Before you start, ask yourself how you will implement your *Commitment to Change*. Start planning stretch-goals quarterly. These stretch goals are goals that are within reach, but can only be obtained through the extension to the limit of what's possible. You can't cross a chasm in two steps. You must stretch to get across.

Decision Making

I'm sure you've noticed, just as psychologists have, that people find it difficult to make decisions if they don't know all the facts. They find it difficult even if they know the missing information is not even particularly relevant. Why is that? What causes the human brain to react to missing facts as a roadblock to obtaining the desired *Commitment to Change*? Sooner or later, a decision must be made.

The key is to make a *Commitment to Change* before the *Status Quo* becomes so painful that a *Commitment to Change* must be made. Still, there are people that will wait to gather facts no matter how irrelevant they are. Fear will keep these people in their *Status Quo* because the *Status Quo* has not become painful enough and the fear of the change is worse than the pain.

When the *Status Quo* does reach that boiling point, people who have waited too long and gathered too many unnecessary facts without working on core issues often make the wrong decision. How many people have been wrapped up in a bad marriage where something could have been done long before a divorce? So many things could have been done before the marriage reached its boiling point. People can be counseled to see the other person's view of things. People can educate themselves about what it takes to be in a happy marriage. They could just finally understand that men and women think vastly different most of the time on different subjects and that the difference in how they think actually builds up a marriage through diversity of thought.

Instead, people often leave. They act as if this life is all there is and they'd better be happy now before they die because there is nothing else. I'm here to tell you…there is something else greater than this life. Yet, people are afraid to die and this fear of death makes them slaves to bad decision-making. This fear of death before they have fully lived causes them to throw away a marriage before they try to change themselves. Wake up! This decision making process will lead to your ruin. Self-justifying psychobabble just causes a bad decision to be a new *Commitment to Change*. Then the matter is worse because a bad decision is looked at as a good change.

Work on yourself first. Stop trying to change the other person. Then you'll be able to build strong and long-lasting relationships.

The Olney Decision Matrix

All of these factors work together to help each of us make better decisions that will have a positive impact on the world around us:

- Bigger Bang for the Buck
- Ease of Implementation
- Available Resources
- Biggest Positive Cost/Benefit
- Fits Best with Purpose/Mission Statement
- Best for Long-Term Success

Unfortunately, thinking about these factors may get a little overwhelming. My dad came up with a decision matrix that simplifies decisions by charting each one and then putting weight to each factor so that we can arrive at the best possible solutions. I can't take credit for this matrix. I just made it look prettier. But I have been using it for my entire business life. It has saved me in certain situations and in one particular instance saved my job. All that a person needs to do is to put multiple decisive factors on the matrix and come up with a factor for each to calculate each decision. This spreadsheet can be found free on my web-site, www.gonatelle.com. I've used this matrix for interviews, projects, vendor decisions, and even a decision as to where to live. Simply plug in a rating from 1 to 10 for each decisive factor and for each decision option. Narrow down your decisions to your top 5 so that you can stay away from analysis paralysis and then see which decision is the closest to 100%. This process will work in nine out of ten decisions if it is done thoughtfully and carefully. While the ratings from 1 to 10 may sometimes be subjective, it does minimize the emotional component. Use it and be prepared to be amazed.

Olney Decision Matrix

Decision Name	Comments	Bigger Bang for the Buck	Ease of Implementation	Available Resources	Biggest Positive Cost/Benefit Analysis	Fits Best with Purpose & Mission Statement	Best for Long-Term Success	Total
Factor ---->		0.15	0.15	0.15	0.15	0.2	0.2	100%
		Rating 1 to 10						
Decision 1								
Decision 2								
Decision 3								
Decision 4								
Decision 5								

Note: Only Change Highlighted Fields

Lessons Learned

When considering your *Commitment to Change*, there are decisive factors that come in to play:

- How much bang you get for your buck
- Ease of implementing your Commitment to Change
- What available resources there are
- Which commitment has the biggest positive Cost/Benefit Analysis
- What fits best with your Purpose/Mission Statements
- What commitment is best for long-term success

There is an Olney Decision Matrix available that puts decisive factors on the matrix to come up with decisions.

A bigger bang for the buck is used in decision-making to describe how much value a decision provides at minimal cost. This can reduce the amount of time we work IN our commitment and instead work ON our commitment. Setting tasks up where they happen automatically improves output and the probability that functions will work with accuracy.

If something is painful, but easy to solve, the decision becomes a no-brainer. The question about what decision to make becomes a little more complicated when you're faced with multiple solutions or options to solve a problem. Nevertheless, if a commitment can be made and waiting would mean an opportunity lost, the decision may be painful, but the conclusion is apparent.

An available resource is something that exists independently that is ready to be consumed so that we can obtain a benefit from it. If the resource is limited or non-renewable, you may have to allocate and manage these resources, but if you don't have resources available at all to you, your decision not to go down a certain path becomes easy.

In order to do a Cost/Benefit Analysis, we must understand the trade-offs in our lives. Every action has an equal and opposite reaction. For every benefit, there is a cost associated with that benefit. When doing a cost/benefit analysis, if the cost of following a certain direction is greater than the benefit (and does not positively affect another benefit), then the direction should not be taken. Consider the risks to your finances and reputation along with the potential loss of not taking your course of action.

Your *Transition Game* starts with a purpose. A purpose is why we're here in the first place. A mission is how we'll get to our *Commitment to Change*. Every step of the decision making process needs to align with the purpose and mission, which will support the vision. The vision is where you're going. A transition may start with a purpose, but a *Commitment to Change* starts with a vision and is completed with a mission. You have to know how you will change to commit to it.

Individuals that are the most successful are those who have a "long time" perspective. The longer the period of time, the more likely those persons will achieve greatness. They are willing to pay the price. There is no discounting the short-term, however, because if you are unable to make it out of the short-term, there will be no long-term. There is pain involved with considering long-term success more important than what we're temporarily going through so a balance needs to be brought between what is worth the pain in the long-term without destroying those important relationships in the short-term.

People find it difficult to make decisions if they don't know all the facts. The human brain reacts to missing facts as a roadblock to obtaining the desired *Commitment to Change*, but sooner or later, a decision must be made. Stop fear from keeping you in your *Status Quo*. When the *Status Quo* reaches a boiling point, people who have waited too long and gathered too many unnecessary facts without working on core issues often make the wrong decision.

Chapter 4
Encouragement

Encouragement

The word "encourage" is interesting. It means to inspire courage. Literally, it is from the Anglo-French word "encorag," which is to put in courage. But where does encouragement come from?

To really appreciate where encouragement comes from, we need to consider how people in the past have been encouraged. Think of these ways:

- **Message Delivery**: a message of encouragement can often be used to spur on a person or team to succeed. The message must come from someone with credentials. In addition, the delivery must have the balance of being crisp, short, and simple in order to inspire courage.

- **Reassurance**: When I've felt awfully helpless, my parents would encourage me by reminding me who they thought I was. Touching me lightly on the shoulder and reassuring me that everything would be all right. Reassurance merely means to restore confidence.

- **Support**: Encouragement comes when someone props you up. Almost as if to come from underneath you and give you sustenance.

- **Recommendation**: I knew when my company GONATELLE was running well. When I had recommendations from one business owner or CEO to another in writing. That recommendation encouraged me and I was welcomed. I wound up being a great help to other organizations, which never would have happened if I hadn't received this encouragement.

- **Confidence**: When someone leads with confidence, the people around them can be in constant struggle, but when the leader urges forward motion with confidence, the people are encouraged.

- **The hard bitter truth**: Winston Churchill gave a broadcast in the 1940's that said:

"In the bitter and increasingly exacting conflict which lies before us we are resolved to keep nothing back, and not to be outstripped by any in service to the common cause. Let the great cities…banish despair even in the midst of their agony. Their liberation is sure. The day will come when the joy-bells will ring again throughout Europe, and when victorious nations, masters not only of their foes but of themselves, will plan and build in justice, in tradition, and in freedom a house of many mansions where there will be room for all."

Churchill didn't sugarcoat the despair. In fact, if you just cut off the first part of this paragraph, this message may have been somewhat depressing. However, he finished what lay ahead with encouragement and strengthening for a better day. Churchill is the one who said "fight before you have to."

- **Care**: Almost everyone knows the saying, "They don't care how much you know until they know how much you care." When someone knows that somebody else cares about them, they are encouraged.

Each of us who is strong in one way or another needs to bear with the failings of the weak and not just to please ourselves. If we take care of and encourage those around us for their own good and build them up, we understand that encouragement might provide hope. Think about these ways that you can encourage others. Encourage others in their:

- Creativity
- Project Management & Completion
- Weight Control
- Exercise Program
- Discovery
- Loss

These are just a few ways. I'm sure you can think of others.

Time with a Mentor

In order to make a strong *Commitment to Change*, it's helpful to have some-one who shares their knowledge with you and imparts their wisdom. The word "Mentor" came from Greek mythology. Mentor was placed in charge of Ulysses' son, Telemachus. This is the same Ulysses who was the hero in Homer's *Odyssey*. Mentor (and those disguised as Mentor) helped Telemachus deal with personal predicaments and sensible goals. In this day and age, a mentor means a counselor who is wise and trusted.

My dad was my mentor before having a mentor became main-stream in the business world. He took the time with me and counseled me. He passed no judgment during our counseling sessions and he gave me wise advice con-tinuously. He said some things that I didn't understand at first…things that I would have to go and research for myself to dig deeper and understand. He taught me the truth. He taught me that truth, in and of itself, does not help or hurt; our action for or against the truth helps or hurts. It is not the truth that sets you free. Knowing the truth sets you free.

You must spend time with your mentor to learn the truth. My dad was a really great dad. He spent a lot of time with me and it never seemed that he wanted to be somewhere else when I was in his presence. We spent a lot of time playing sports or having a meal together. Every morning in Junior High School (now called Middle School) and High School before I started to drive, he adjusted his work schedule to drop me off. I would kiss him good-bye each morning. One morning, he commented that I didn't have to kiss him goodbye if it made me uncomfortable in front of the other kids and I remember commenting back that nobody ever bothered me about it. It probably helped being the super-intense big kid in class. Nobody usually bothers that kid. I wouldn't trade that time with him, though. We built a relationship that I take with me wherever I go. He and I don't agree on all things, but we talk out differences and research our thoughts so that I don't follow blindly.

My dad taught me not to just "take his word for it." He is the one who taught me to know where I came from. He taught me to know what I'm good at, know what I'm not good at, enhance what I'm good at, and minimize what I'm not good at. He taught me to intentionally and deliberately work through a transition until the *Commitment to Change* occurs. A mentor will teach you that wisdom is mating reason with knowledge.

Here are several sayings that I've written through the years as we had our time together. More insight to this man will be given in my future books and have already been written in my prior book, *The Transition Game*:

Wisdom of my Dad

- Only a moment in time can be experienced. Once it's gone, it's gone. Remember the past and look forward to the future, but live in the present.
- Time grows in the past and diminishes in the future in relation to the beginning.
- God gives us 3 things:
  ○ Life
  ○ Choice, and
  ○ A conscience to deal with that choice
- Don't try to punch holes in what someone is saying while they're talking. Rather, pick out the good things about what they're saying.
- You can't have satisfaction without experience.
- It's not what the parents do, but who they are that help children grow.
- You can have a personal and long lasting effect on someone with an unexpected compliment that is timely and honest.
- Lack of honesty attacks the credibility of everything else in someone's life. When you overemphasize something that's not true, everything you say isn't credible.
- Equal rights are not just equal rights. Equal rights are equal responsibility.
- Marriage appears to be a game, but it's not a game. The rules have to be flexible and we need to understand that "marriage rules" are there to take care of us together.
- Marriage must be like a negotiation. Both sides have to win. Win-Lose or Lose-Win turns in to Lose-Lose in the long run.
- "Adjustment" is adapting to change. Adjustment is not "change"; of course, change may not always involve adjustment because the committed part may never have to be brought into conformity with that change.
- Compassion, caring, and altruism are necessary for love.

My dad is a brilliant man. There were times that I would need to research something thoroughly to understand what he was talking about. When he would talk to me about minimizing uncontrolled change & maximizing controlled change, he would analogize it to the Bessemer process of making hard steel from pig iron. That pushed me to figure out what the Bessemer process was. It occurs when high-pressure oxygen is blown into molten iron to get rid of the impurities in a very controlled way. The knowledge of the Bessemer process (replaced by the "basic oxygen process" for even more control) is less important than realizing that what my dad said about maximizing controlled change was the truth.

I can remember speedily writing at times because my dad would often say things that were precious gems that I would cherish. Mentors will trigger noble character in the protégé that truly seeks the right *Commitment to Change*. This protégé receives the message with great eagerness and then examines it to see if what was said is true. As a result, the protégé will believe the point of the message.

Sacking Out and the Bystander Effect

People experiencing the Bystander Effect don't make good decisions. In 2010, the news kept replaying a video of a man saving a woman from a mugging in New York. The mugger turned on the man and stabbed him. What happened next was horrifying. As the man lay on the sidewalk bleeding to death, people walked by and disregarded him. One individual turned the man over and took account of the blood. Then he turned the man back over and calmly walked away. Nobody called for help.

It's as if the people were frozen with inaction. My daughter has a Psychology degree and she told me that the people in New York were experiencing the Bystander Effect. The bystanders gave up personal responsibility and replaced it with social influence. Since "nobody" was doing anything about this situation, it must not be necessary for "anyone" to do anything. The bystanders' inaction may have happened because they couldn't determine the appropriate way to act.

Now, let me talk about "Sacking Out." This term describes what was done to horses in the past to desensitize them. This old-school technique used sacks of cans tied to the horse's saddle, whereby the horse would be "wrecked" by the constant run while attempting to get away from the perceived noisy danger that would never go away.

Desensitization of some sort is necessary to keep a horse and the people around them safe. However, there are ways to desensitize horses without ruining them. Using methods such as brushing, touching, bathing, and picking up the horse's hoof prove very effective especially when the horses are approached at a younger age. Unfortunately, many abusive practices still occur. Individuals who perform "earing down" on rowdy horses, twist or bite the horse's ear until they submit. Better tools can be used to get each horse to apply the correct behavior.

Left to our own devices, though, without an intentional, deliberate, and good process, a wrong end will be ensured. This wrong end will guarantee someone who is mentally "off"…just like the people that let that New York man die in the street.

Lessons Learned

The word "encourage" means to inspire courage or to put in courage. Consider how people have encouraged others through message delivery, reassurance, support, recommendation, confidence, and the hard bitter truth. A message of encouragement can often be used to spur on a person or team to succeed, but the message must come from someone with credentials. Encouragement comes when someone props you up. We wind up being a great help to others because of encouraging support that we've received. When someone leads with confidence, the people around them are encouraged. We all need to finish the hard bitter truth with encouragement and strengthening for a better day.

Each of us who is strong in one way or another needs to bear with the failings of the weak and not just to please ourselves. If we take care of and encourage those around us for their own good to build them up, encouragement provides hope.

In order to make a strong *Commitment to Change*, it is helpful to have someone who shares their knowledge with you and imparts their wisdom. A mentor is a counselor who is wise and trusted. Knowing the truth sets you free. You must spend time with your mentor to learn the truth. They will teach you not to "take their word for it."

People experiencing the Bystander Effect don't make good decisions. People become frozen with inaction. They give up personal responsibility and replace it with social influence. Since "nobody" is doing anything about this situation, it must not be necessary for "anyone" to do anything. We can become "wrecked" by the constant run while attempting to get away from the perceived danger that never goes away. Desensitization may be necessary sometimes, but there are ways to become desensitized without ruining ourselves. Many abusive practices still occur in business, families, and sports and better tools, like this book, can be used so that people can apply correct behaviors. Left to our own devices without an intentional, deliberate, and good process, a wrong end is guaranteed.

THE SECOND C:
Certainty

Chapter 5
Fully Convinced

Fully Convinced

Be fully convinced of your *Commitment to Change*. Many people may have sought the same *Commitment to Change* in the past and failed because it was handed down from someone else and they were not fully convinced that it was a good and right change. With this in mind, carefully investigate the change and then plan an orderly process for that change. Then you will be fully convinced of the things you were told.

Sometimes when the bad guys are winning, the *Commitment to Change* may waiver. There is no full certainty when wavering occurs. The wavering person is not fully convinced. Be certain of this: Justice will prevail. It may seem like the bad guys are winning now, but your work will not be forgotten. Show the same diligence to the very end so that what you hope for can be fully realized. Don't become lazy, but instead imitate those that have obtained the dream through their faith and patience.

So…what will it take for someone to be fully convinced? What does it take to be persuaded or assured that this particular *Commitment to Change* is right?…and why is being fully convinced so important to this change? Of course, when there is a clear path, it's easier to be fully convinced, but fear and lack of focus will work against clarity. You have to continue down that path knowing that, despite the fog, no weapon formed real or unreal against you will do well. This *Commitment to Change* must be sharply defined as to be free of cloudiness or obscurity.

Being fully convinced means your mind has been made up so that no matter which way you turn, the change will be made. You've locked yourself in. There's no going back. You may be torn between two paths in order to get to your destination. One way may seem better by far, but it may be more necessary to take another path so that progress may be surer and the celebration more complete on account of you. Whichever way you go to the new change, of which you are fully convinced, conduct yourself in a manner that is consistent with standing firm.

All In

What is your *Commitment to Change*? What is it? What do you want to change? What Status Quo do you want to leave? What good thing are you seeking? Are you seeking this *Commitment to Change* wholeheartedly? Are you "all in"?

If you're not "all in," then you don't want whatever "it" is as much as is necessary. If you're not "all in," you're just going through the motions to look good when your heart really isn't in it. Excuse the poker term "all in," but it aptly fits when a player puts all they have in the pot because he or she doesn't have any more stake in the game. Once a player is "all in," they can call every bet and stay in for the remainder of the deal. They show their heart. It's a heart thing. A good heart is "all in"…wholeheartedly. Where you put all your chips is where your heart is. What you pay attention to grows.

Cheating at cards is wicked and it's not "all in." Making a *Commitment to Change* with a good heart earns a sure reward rather than deceptive wages. Hasty decisions are not "all in." People that are quick with their mouth are not "all in." A lot of words just mark the speech of fools. Instead, have confidence. A discerning heart that can distinguish between right and wrong is a mark of leadership. The only way to do anything great is to be "all in."

When you're playing cards, you must do everything the pit-boss tells you to do. But play cards, just like you would make that *Commitment to Change*, sincerely with all of your heart…not only when the pit-boss's eye is on you or to curry their favor. You're not "all in" if you're only playing fair when the dealer or the pit-boss is looking.

Double-Minded

What does it mean to be double-minded? I talked a little about it in my last book, *The Transition Game*, when I discussed the trapeze artist and stated that flexibility comes when the circumstances change. The goal may still remain the same, but if the circumstances change, it may require letting go of something instead of holding on.

Being double-minded is the act of letting go of something to get to a goal, but still holding on so that obtaining the goal is not possible. This could happen in reverse. In order to get to a goal, it may require holding on tight to your values. A double-minded person lets go of their values, which keeps them from their goals.

Being double-minded is having an undecided, wavering opinion. There is no true *Commitment to Change* with a double-minded person. Someone who will go with the flow or stay the course as long as they won't get blamed for anything is double-minded. That person plays a game of talking out loud and arguing both sides so that if anything does go wrong, they can say, "Hey. I brought up that opinion, but nobody listened to me."

All that being double-minded accomplishes is deflection of blame for a time. It won't last forever. Blame will fall back on the double-minded person eventually. Of course, unless there is complete denial, double-minded people must ultimately live with themselves. And that's a fate worse than blame.

Lessons Learned

It's more difficult to have a true *Commitment to Change* if it's handed down from someone else. We must each carefully investigate our change so we can be fully convinced that it is good and right. *Commitment to Change* may waiver when events are going badly, but there is no full certainty when this wavering occurs. Show diligence and don't become lazy. Instead, imitate those that have obtained the dream through their faith and patience.

When there is a clear path, it's easier to be fully convinced, but fear and lack of focus will work against clarity. *Commitment to Change* must be sharply defined as to be free of cloudiness or obscurity. Being fully convinced means your mind has been made up so that no matter which way you turn, the change will be made. You've locked yourself in. Once someone is "all in," they show their heart. And a good heart is wholehearted.

Hasty or cheating decisions are not "all in." People that are quick with their mouth are not "all in." Instead, have confidence with a discerning heart that can distinguish between right and wrong. That's a mark of leadership. The only way to do anything great is to be "all in" and you're NOT "all in" if you're only playing fair when someone is looking.

Your goal may still remain the same, but if the circumstances change, it may require letting go of something instead of holding on. In order to get to a goal, it may require holding on tight to your values. A double-minded person lets go of their values, which keeps them from their goals. Being double-minded is having an undecided, wavering opinion. There is no true *Commitment to Change* with a double-minded person who stays the course as long as they don't get blamed. Being double-minded deflects blame for a time, but that won't last forever. No matter what, each of us must live with ourselves…whether we're double-minded or fully convinced.

Chapter 6
Emotional Decisions

Emotional Decisions

Making a decision just because "it just feels right" will get you in trouble. We tend to trick ourselves into decisions that will feel good in the short-term, but get us into longer term danger.

It may not be a bad thing that emotions cause the decision-making process to start in the first place, but after that starting-process begins, your self-control must take over. Emotions may spur you on to get out of the *Status Quo*. Your emotions may even generate options so you can exit a painful situation. But if you don't use some type of logic in the decision-*making* component, you may be jumping out of the frying pan into the fire. You may be leaving a painful *Status Quo* for an even more painful future.

However, using emotions in the proper context and with the right motivation can be a very valuable tool. Even the simple decisions are difficult if emotions don't play a part. If we ignore the fight, flight, freeze responses, we are headed for failure. A high Emotional Intelligence allows good decision-making through:

- Perception
- Generation
- Understanding
- Managing

Perception – Emotional Intelligence begins with the ability to have awareness of your emotions and the emotions of those around you. Seldom will any of us come to win-win solutions if we don't collect the clues to our own emotions and the emotions of those around us. We have to be able to perceive emotions in the first place to lay a foundation for using, understanding, and managing them to meet goals.

Generation – Emotional Intelligence generates and uses emotion based on each situation. You may have seen actors cry on queue. That may be a fringe example, but they are generating tears, an emotion, based on the character that they're playing. They are properly using emotions by generating them. I'm not suggesting that anyone be false about their emotions. Part of Emotional Intelligence is being genuine with each of our emotions. All that I am suggesting is that you can create good habits by using the right mood for the right situation. The word "happy" comes from the 14th century and has the same derivative word as "happening." "Hap" simply means "chance or luck." Based on the original meaning of the word, we really do not deserve to be happy. If we deserve something, then we've earned it. If we deserve something, then it was by our own merit that we gained it. If emotions are based on what is happening around us (events that we may or may not have control of), self-control is limited and Emotional Intelligence decreases. However, we can choose to use the right emotion and generate feelings so that we are not controlled by what's happening around us.

Understanding – Answering questions about how we feel helps us understand ourselves better and gives us an understanding of what makes each of us tick. If I'm "feeling" happy, it is my goal to find out why I'm feeling happy so I can replicate that emotion in situations that may call for that emotion and in which "I'm just not feeling it." This understanding gives us insight and knowledge into our own souls and makes us self-aware. Quite frankly, if there isn't emotional knowledge and insight, then we won't understand the people around us. We won't be able to empathize. And we definitely won't be able to match the right emotion with the right circumstance.

Managing – I'm sure we've all met a socially inept person who can't manage their emotions. They're so consumed with themselves that they engage in self-talk about reality when they have no concept of what reality really means. Managing emotions breaks us out of our self-absorbed nature and seeks, instead, to learn from emotions and take appropriate action based on the information gained. This valuable information can then be used to solve problems so that a great *Commitment to Change* can be realized.

The higher the Emotional Intelligence, the greater the possibility of making good decisions by perceiving our own emotions and the emotions of others as well as harnessing those emotions to solve the problem of the *Status Quo*. After perceiving and using emotions, we begin to detect the slightest changes in emotion in ourselves and others and then we can regulate them so we can get to our goals and the goals of those around us.

Using Emotional Intelligence wraps logic and emotion together to come up with the best possible solution. If you only use emotions in your decisions because something "just feels right," you will be destined to fail. In 1990, Peter Salovey and John D. Mayer defined Emotional Intelligence as "the subset of social intelligence that involves the ability to monitor one's own and others' feelings and emotions, to discriminate among them and to use this information to guide one's thinking and actions." That provides perspective as to where emotions belong in your *Commitment to Change*.

Optimism

Optimism comes from the word optimize, which is a mathematical selection of the best part from a group of available options. The search for options is very important, but the right selection of those options is paramount. Optimism is largely a learned trait, but some people seem to innately look at the bright side of things. Optimistic people may go through the same difficulties as pessimistic people, but the results are better with less stress. Of course, we can be overly optimistic. I've told people that I was with a company that had the most over-optimistic groupthink label written all over it and the company failed because of it. But optimistic people don't worry. They know that we can't add a single hour to our lives by worrying. We all have 86,400 seconds in a day. Ralph Waldo Emerson said to, "work joyfully and peacefully, knowing that right thoughts and right efforts will inevitably bring about right results and not escape the reward."

Optimism isn't denial of the bad things in life. Optimism is the realization of the best parts of life despite the bad parts. Sometimes you have an adversary and sometimes that adversary is useful to fight against. Resistance is what makes a boat sail. You can look at wind-resistance as an obstruction or you can look at wind-resistance as a way to get to your goal. You must make your *Commitment to Change* with gusto. Those who sow sparingly will reap sparingly, and whoever sows generously will also reap generously.

You have to start any process by saying, "I want to look back at this event and know that I did the best I could regardless of the outcome." Too often, we get into the heat of the battle and it gets too hard. We get pessimistic and we forget our purpose. Whatever or whoever the enemy is, they seem too strong for us. Everything seems to be going well for them and not for us. Well, the same sun shines on your enemy and we certainly cannot fight the sun. Should we accept good and not trouble?

Opportunity involves a favorable time or condition for doing something, but it's only an opportunity if you recognize it. Optimism helps you realize that opportunity has two components: A favorable condition AND action. Optimism and opportunity combined help us focus on what we CAN change. If we have no control of a problem, then it's not really a problem. If we're caught in an earthquake, we have the control to get ourselves under a table, but we don't have control of the ground shaking. Optimism allows you to go toward your Commitment to Change despite any suffering it produces. The optimistic person knows that they can persevere through this suffering. This perseverance produces character, which produces hope... and that hope does not disappoint. My good friend, Joe Lawson, always says, "I have many things to think about, but nothing to worry about."

Lessons Learned

Decisions that will feel good in the short-term, but get us into longer term danger are trouble. After emotions cause the decision-making process to start, self-control must take over. Emotions often spur us on to get out of the Status Quo and generate options to get out of a painful situation. But there must be logic in the decision-*making* component. Using emotions in the proper context and with the right motivation can be a valuable tool.

In this chapter we talked about Emotional Intelligence that allows good decision-making through Perception, Generation, Understanding, and Managing. Emotional Intelligence begins with the ability to perceive our emotions. We must collect these clues and lay a foundation for using, understanding, and managing emotions to meet our goals. Each of us can properly use emotions without falsifying them and create good habits by using the right mood for the right situation. Contrary to popular belief, we don't deserve to be happy. We don't deserve something when we don't earn it or bring it about by our own merit. We can choose to use the right emotion and generate feelings so that we are not controlled by what's happening around us, though.

It is extremely important to understand how we feel and why we feel a certain way. In that way, we can recreate emotions in situations that may call for that emotion. Understanding in this way gives us insight and knowledge so we can understand the people around us and empathize. Once we understand our emotions, managing emotions breaks us out of our self-absorbed nature to take appropriate action based on the information gained.

The higher the Emotional Intelligence, the greater the possibility of making good decisions. We can regulate emotions so that we can get to our goals and the goals of those around us. Using this Emotional Intelligence wraps logic and emotion together to come up with the best possible solution. Emotional Intelligence is defined as "the subset of social intelligence that involves the ability to monitor one's own and others' feelings and emotions, to discriminate among them and to use this information to guide one's thinking and actions."

Optimism comes from the word optimize, which is a mathematical selection of the best part from a group of available options. The search for options is very important, but the right selection of those options is paramount. We can't add a single hour to our lives by worrying. Choosing the right option eliminates worry. Optimism is not the denial of the bad things in life. It's just the realization of the best parts of life despite the bad parts. Opportunity is a favorable time or condition for doing something, BUT it's only an opportunity if you recognize it. Optimism is the intersection of a favorable condition and doing something about it. I may have many things to think about, but nothing to worry about.

Chapter 7
Approach

Approach

I encountered a situation with a normally creative employee that was having a problem being imaginative. This person's creativity was stifled by a superior when they brought up new ideas. Their ideas were continuously rejected and altered. As a result, creativity was not rewarded so it did not get repeated. What gets rewarded gets repeated. In order that we might find the best possible solution, two things needed to change: First, the approach of the creative employee, and second, the approach of the receiver.

The creative employee needed to change their approach to be more confident and self-assured and the receiver needed to change their approach to allow mistakes so that we could find the best possible solution. I was reminded of a player on my son's baseball team who was in a life-long hitting slump. I could tell that he was big and strong so I told him that all he needed to do was to get his bat on the ball and see what would happen. I asked him not to "kill it" when he swung the bat. I just wanted him to get his bat on the ball. He didn't need to try and swing for the fence each time. It was just important to get his bat on the ball. When he did this, he would hit with ease. The joy he felt consistently getting on base replaced the depression that he previously felt by sitting on the bench after each at-bat.

This was the first season that he was on my son's team and what we realized that none of his previous coaches had spent any time with him because if they had him on their team, they always had a fall-guy. Some coaches would blame losses on him. Other coaches had a fill-in which essentially meant that the players the coach favored (who weren't necessarily the best players) didn't have to sit out any innings because they had a ready-made bench-warmer. Nobody would fault the coach for sitting a player on the bench who couldn't hit so the coach was free to ignore him and not feel any pressure to do his job, which was to coach the player up.

It's all in the approach. To approach a problem is to begin work on it. To approach a problem is to make advances and to set about addressing that problem. When we approach a problem, we are not ignoring it. We are seeking to solve it. That's why approach is so important. You must approach any problem with all of the following 4 criteria:

1. **Quality:** You must approach a problem with a degree of excellence and competence. If you are not competent, quality will not be long-lasting and if your approach is not exceptional, you will not excel.
2. **Character:** You must approach a problem with honesty, courage, and integrity in order to face and overcome problems.
3. **Attitude:** Attitude is closely related to character and you must approach any issue in the proper manner with a good and positive disposition.
4. **Timeliness:** Problems that are ignored are problems that will continue. Problems must be approached in a timely manner so the problematic circumstance can be corrected before it grows out of control.

If we don't approach problems with these 4 attributes in mind, then we really don't want to solve the problem. The pain of the problem (*Status Quo*) isn't really that bad. If our approach is off or a step is missing, it means we really don't care. That sounds extremely harsh, doesn't it? Think about the last problem or issue that you have had. Has your approach been off? Is one of the preceding steps missing? Think about if you had really cared about fixing the problem. Would you have included one of those missing steps? Better yet, will you go back now, admit that you were wrong by missing a step, and fix an old problem that still exists? I dare you to do so!

Vigilance

To be vigilant is to be awake and alert. Being vigilant is the opposite of being asleep at the wheel. Being vigilant is being watchful and aware of risks that might sideswipe you. This is a dangerous world that doesn't really care about you and it takes someone with vigilance to navigate the rough roads it sometimes provides. Being vigilant doesn't mean being a vigilante who takes the law into their own hands. Being vigilant is being controlled by one's conscience according to some moral code. It is being led by a "weltanschauung," which is each of our own personal philosophies or our world-view. This world-view must be approached with humbleness, but your cares must be cast away at the same time. It's a sobering thought that this world is waiting for you to slip up. It's almost as if it seeks to devour you. It will devour the outliers first. Think of a wolf-pack attacking a herd of sheep. The attack first comes to the stragglers on the outside of the herd. If you're not awake and alert to the dangers of the wolves out there, you could be eaten up by the negative environment around you. Heaven help the people that are disconnected from any type of networking in business. They will have the hardest time finding a new job if they are ever laid-off. The disconnected stragglers are easier for this world to pick off.

There is a particular steadfastness with vigilance through suffering that won't last as long if you don't run away from it. When we're not vigilant, we continue in a painful *Status Quo*. The term "weather eye" came from being vigilant and diligent. It was a nautical term for someone remaining alert, but still carrying on other activities at the same time. We must do certain things in this world to survive, but we don't need to consume ourselves with those activities. There is a balance that comes when we occupy our time with something that doesn't consume us. Keeping a "weather eye" means we stay alert, but are balanced at the same time.

Remission and indolence are enemies of vigilance. Indolence is a word that causes little pain, but dislikes the work and effort of vigilance. It's lazy and idle. It settles with the inertia of this world. If you've read my previous book, *"The Transition Game: What I didn't know that cost me my job, my marriage, and my peace of mind,"* we learned that inertia is a word that means idle or lazy. Inertia says that objects at rest tend to stay at rest and objects in motion tend to stay in motion. Essentially, objects and people will keep with the *Status Quo*. They keep doing what they're doing. Indolence is insensitivity to pain when someone is hardened by the *Status Quo* and against moral influences. They are left with a strong inclination for the *Status Quo*. They don't realize how awful the *Status Quo* is and they don't respect any new *Commitment to Change* or appreciate the rescue that it provides. They don't even fear the repercussions that will happen when they stay where they are. Remission of the *Status Quo* when you remain in the *Status Quo* is pardoning bad behavior. Remission can be a good thing when the *Status Quo* dissolves, but too often people stay in the *Status Quo* and explain it away as if it's not happening. They stop their treatment before the *Commitment to Change* is fully realized and become more immersed in the *Status Quo* than they were before. Be vigilant so this doesn't happen to you.

Lessons Learned

It's all in the approach. We must begin work on a problem, make advances, and set about addressing that problem. When we approach a problem, we don't ignore it. We seek to solve it. Any problem must be approached with quality, character, attitude, and timeliness. Quality is the degree of excellence and competence. Character includes honesty, courage, and integrity. Attitude is approaching any issue in the proper manner with a good and positive disposition. Timeliness happens when problems are approached before they grow out of control. If we don't approach problems with these four attributes in mind, then we really don't want to solve the problem.

To be vigilant is to be awake and alert. It is being watchful and aware of risks. Being vigilant is being controlled with humbleness by one's conscience according to some moral code. A negative environment can eat us up if we're disconnected stragglers. There is a particular steadfastness with vigilance through suffering that won't last as long if you don't run away from it. It takes that "weather eye" to remain alert while carrying on other activities at the same time. There is a balance that comes when we occupy our time with something that doesn't consume us.

Remission and indolence are enemies of vigilance. Indolence is insensitivity to pain when someone is hardened by the *Status Quo* and against moral influences. Remission of the *Status Quo* when you remain in the *Status Quo* is pardoning bad behavior. Remission can be a good thing when the *Status Quo* dissolves, but too often people stay in the *Status Quo* and explain it away as if it's not happening.

Chapter 8
The Reasonable Person

The Reasonable Person Test

Historically, this has been called the 'reasonable man test', but 'man' should be relabeled 'mankind," which refers to both men and women. It's a test of common law, which looks at an objective standard by which our individual conduct can be measured. It guides how we act vs. what a reasonable person would do in the same situation. A good question to ask ourselves when we're confronted with a problem or need help with any solution is, "What would a reasonable person do in this situation?"

In order to be reasonable, there must be sound judgment based on moderation where extremes are avoided. Excesses cause reasonableness to fly out the window. Humanity is prone to excesses. Rather, being moldable and pliant to the right *Commitment to Change* (not the wrong one) means that we moderate ourselves. If we aren't moldable and pliant, we won't look ahead toward the right *Commitment to Change* and we could become that proverbial pillar of salt. Similarly, a farmer isn't worth his salt if he looks back when he puts his hands to the plow. The farmer must look forward to tread a straight furrow.

To become reasonable, we need to be planted firmly in good soil. We have all seen news stories about people snapping. They commit unreasonable acts because their environment has become such that they have hit the extremes. Everything might be going wrong for this person and if they are not rooted firmly enough, the winds of life will snap them like a twig.

Here's the key: If you've grown up in an unreasonable environment or an extreme environment does not make it easy to be reasonable, graft yourself into a new environment. Become a new person. Nobody says that you are tied to your old way of life with the extremes it exhibits. Grafted branches are actually sturdier because of the graft. You can become sturdy. You can become reasonable. Avoid extremes and excesses in your life that would draw you away from the right *Commitment to Change* and live a life that is reasonable and true and good.

It Can Be This Good

There is something in most of us that just can't believe things can be this good. When a woman has a man that cherishes her, she may secretly sabotage the relationship because something this good is scary. This woman may not realize her value. When a man holds on to his old hurtful ways instead of running to the woman that cares for him, he only hurts himself. He holds on to his old ways because he just doesn't believe it can be this good and a woman would care for him this much. He doesn't realize his value.

Unfortunately, not realizing that something can be as good as it is becomes a downward spiral that can start with just one person. It moves from a spiral to a straight down trajectory if both people in the relationship do the wrong thing. Someone may think:

- "I don't deserve this."
- "I'm not valuable enough to receive something like this."
- "If it's too good to be true, it's not true."
- "The other person can't be looking out for my better welfare. Nobody else has ever done that."
- "The other person has the wrong motivations."

It's almost like digging at wounds that aren't there. Digging at something that's not there creates a wound of its own. Examples of people digging at wounds that aren't there are Adult Children of Alcoholics (ACA) who will misunderstand what normal is and use fantasy as a tool. At the first sign of trouble an ACA will cut and run and not follow through on their promises. They don't understand that "it can be this good" because their life has been filled with difficulty and they, as children, never came first.

The core breakdown of this mentality is the inability to have fun. When there is a lack of fun, everything is approached with seriousness and true intimacy is foreign. At the same time, though, intimacy is sought and overreacting emotions seesaw. Closeness with another person is lost. In the worst cases, an ACA will attack their partner without giving serious consideration to the consequences. Actions become so impulsive that control vanishes and the clean-up becomes insurmountable.

This brief and oversimplified description of an Adult Child of an Alcoholic is how many of us act when we don't believe that it really "can be this good." We project negative meaning into something that's not there. If you find yourself saying, "I know what you're thinking," stop yourself. You probably don't know what the other person is thinking. Stop being like an ACA that sabotages their relationships. Instead, accept what good comes your way while holding on to the core principles that make you who you are.

Pain

I've said it before and I will say it again: "The avoidance of pain sells better than the pursuit of pleasure." If you're running a marketing campaign, you'll want to show how your product or service will alleviate pain rather than give pleasure. People who are addicted to pornography are masking some type of pain. They're not necessarily seeking pleasure unless pleasure is the way to get away from their pain. Spurs dig into a horse to get it to run at the rider's pace. This is a painful process for the horse. In fact, the horse is just trying to get away from pain.

Still, we should spur one another on and pain may be involved in that process. Pain tells you that the *Status Quo* should be re-evaluated. It's important to recognize pain and why it's there in the first place. Pain can be useful. In addition, depending on the type of pain, the remedy is applied in different fashions. Pain from arthroscopic surgery, which is minimally invasive, has a remedy far different than that of major organ surgery. Someone's pain threshold may be high and the pain might be similar for small and large pain, but the commitment to the cure may be completely different.

Recognizing the stage that pain exists can reveal what to do with it. The pain from the *Status Quo* may mean getting away from it while the pain from "Doing What it Takes"[2] may mean working through it. Pain is important and the complete avoidance of pain is probably not good. If you've gone through "Deciding if it's Important enough to do what it Takes" [2], pain may be just what the doctor ordered.

Pain is part of our defense system and the intensity of pain tells you just how important it is. Unfortunately, we live in a world where pain is part of our everyday life. Our bodies were designed to be optimal, but outside and inside forces cause damage to this original design. When our defenses are low, pain finds its way in…causing us to increase our defenses or remove ourselves from the *Status Quo*. The funny bone is actually a nerve. In fact, it is the largest unprotected and undefended nerve in our bodies. It runs from our shoulder down to our little finger and hitting our funny bone isn't so funny.

My dad has said that all problems come from someone trying to alleviate pain or perceived pain. Similarly, all achievements come from someone trying to alleviate pain or perceived pain. The difference is the choice you make.

It's interesting that we've just recapped what holds people back and what may make them go in the wrong direction. What might hold someone back is that their *Status Quo* may not be painful enough. Scott Strong from a company called Safety Services says exactly that,

> "We being mere men will wait to do the right thing until we are confronted or a crisis demands that we act. If we continue to present the solution to a problem that hasn't yet occurred then hopefully at some point in time we will heed the advice of those wiser and eliminate the problem before it even occurs."

Lessons Learned

Historically, a 'reasonable man test' would guide how we act vs. what a reasonable person would do. In order to be reasonable, there must be sound judgment based on moderation where extremes are avoided. Excess works against being moldable and pliant to the right *Commitment to Change*. It may be difficult, but necessary, to graft ourselves into a new environment after someone has grown up in a less than desirable extreme. That doesn't make it easy to be reasonable. Nevertheless, nobody is tied to their old way of life.

When someone subtly sabotages a good relationship because they don't believe that it can be truly good, they may not realize their own value.

We only hurt ourselves when we don't realize our value. If you have ever felt that "I don't deserve this" or "I'm not valuable enough to receive something like this," then think again. This is a self-defeating attitude. Digging at a wound that's not there will cause a wound of its own. When actions become impulsive, control vanishes and clean-up becomes insurmountable. It really "can be this good." Instead of reading negative meaning into something that's not there, accept what good comes your way while holding on to the core principles that make you who you are.

Avoidance of pain sells better than the pursuit of pleasure. People don't seek pleasure, necessarily, unless pleasure is the way to get away from their pain. Still, pain tells you that the *Status Quo* should be re-evaluated. It's important to recognize pain and why it's there in the first place. Pain can be useful. Depending on the type of pain, the remedy is applied in different fashions. Recognizing the stage that pain exists can reveal why it's there in the first place. Pain is important and the complete avoidance of pain is not good. Pain is part of our defense system and the intensity of pain tells us just how important it is. All problems come from someone trying to alleviate pain or perceived pain. Similarly, all achievements come from someone trying to alleviate pain or perceived pain. The difference is the choice you make.

THE THIRD C:
Charter

THE THIRD C Charter

Chapter 9
Values

Own Your Own VALUES

In order to realize a true *Commitment to Change*, you must have your own VALUES as they are listed below:

V-alidation (valid plan or validity)
A-ppraisal (verification or verifiable results)
L-ook (view)
U-tterance (voice)
E-yes (vision)
S-ense (values)

"I want to feel validated." How many of you have heard this statement or have said it yourselves? Granted, this statement is a starting point to finding validity, but what people may not notice is that seeking validation means that someone is seeking to be made valid. This need for **validation** by saying, "I just want to feel validated" is the same as a person saying, "I just want to be made valid." It's as if the person saying this doesn't realize that they have already produced the desired result. They don't understand that their life is already valuable…that they are already valuable. I'm here to tell you that you are already valuable. Understanding this is really the starting point to finding validity. Fully grasping that you are valuable will get you to the next step and past the mire of seeking to be made valid. You are already there.

You should always start a process by gauging what your desired results will be. This **appraisal** process will determine your success rate. If you don't know how to gauge results, it's the same as acting like Alice in Wonderland when Alice asked the Cheshire Cat if he could help her find her way. I mentioned in my last book, *The Transition Game*, that the Cheshire Cat said in response, "well that depends on where you want to get to." Alice replied, "Oh, it really doesn't matter…" "Then it really doesn't matter which way you go" answered the cat.

If you don't have an appraisal process, you won't have verifiable results. Then you are really just wandering.

Once you're done wandering, you'll need to set your own sights. This is another way of understanding that we are seeking, investigating, searching for, examining, and inquiring to make sure we're starting down the path. We must have our own *look*!

Only after we study and look for our direction can we use our own voice and announce each of our own *Commitments to Change*. This **utterance** is what we use to articulate our decisions with precision and make them known. This may be the hardest step for people to take because to have one's own voice is scary. Public speaking is the number one fear in today's society for a reason. People may not necessarily want to own their own direction. *Commitment to Change* voyeurs have become commonplace because it's easy to recycle words and not own your own voice. There will be no real *Commitment to Change*, though, if you just repeat what sounds good without researching for yourself. Even if it's the right thing to do, you may still fall off the right path if something better-sounding comes along.

In order to see where you're going, you must passionately own your vision. There is something good about seeing the evidence and destination with our own *eyes*. There is something noble about doing your own exploration and not believing something just "because someone said so." I've told people that I've taught not to, necessarily, believe me when I speak. I want them to see the evidence with their own eyes. I want them to come to their own conclusions and figure out their own *Commitment to Change*.

My daughter, Danielle, graduated Cum Laude from Cal Baptist with her degree in Psychology, but perhaps a more important award that she received when she was in grade school was the "Common Sense" award from her school Principal. I wouldn't trade in her degree and, I'm sure, she wouldn't either, but the Common Sense award was more important to me because, frankly, common sense isn't common and the people that have common sense wind up figuring out the right way to get things done. My daughter always had sense about her. Common *sense* is using all of the common faculties (sight, hearing, smell, taste, or touch) to perceive a stimulus.

This stimulus is something that could be generated from inside or outside the body, but it is a catalyst for a *Commitment to Change* and we need to own our sense to arrive at the destination. Your VALUES must not be someone else's. Each person must find their own.

The Ends Do NOT Justify the Means

When someone says the words, "the ends justify the means," they are expressing the view that something wrong (the "means") can be right (justified) simply because the outcome (the "ends") works out. To justify something or someone is to show that they are right. When somebody states that the ends justify the means, they're actually saying that a good result makes the way you got there right regardless if the way you got to the result was right or wrong. Essentially, they're saying what is wrong may be right. That statement is neither logical nor correct. The rightness of an action is not based on the outcome.

All sorts of inconsistencies can be wrought by the thinking that something morally wrong can be morally right just because it ends well. On the flip-side, there are actions that may appear to be wrong on the surface that are actually just and right. Fighting may be considered wrong at the surface, but fighting against evil would be right. Killing may be considered wrong, but killing an animal that is about to harm a group of people would be right.

Conversely, many people hold to the idea that the ends do not justify the means with a tight and narrow view. They hold on to this view so tightly that they will allow themselves to be physically or metaphorically murdered just so they don't kill anyone else. Allowing themselves to be physically or metaphorically murdered without any struggle is committing murder. It just happens to be suicide. This scenario describes someone so focused on the means that they disregard the end. That's not right either.

You can slip around all these arguments by saying that there really is no right or wrong. What's right for you is okay. You're not allowed to make a judgment call on what I do. That's ridiculous. Plainly, there are right-wrong, win-lose, good-bad decisions. If you've ever made decisions, you know how those decisions cause results, good or bad, based on that choice.

There is an old story based on a prostitute named Rahab who hid some Israeli spies. She lied to their pursuers and misled them. Her protection of the spies was credited as a right decision. The correct decision she made didn't come because she lied or misled anyone, but because she protected someone. I've made the case with this story that there probably was a way for her not to lie or mislead anyone AND she could have protected the spies. The fact that she obtained a good result didn't justify her choice to lie or mislead. However, her decision to protect the Israeli spies was considered a right decision. She may still have had to pay a price for her bad means (just because she's a human being), even though she obtained an ideal ending.

Attach Yourself to the Right Approach & Detach Yourself from the Outcome

Okay, you've come all this way and now I'm telling you to detach yourself from the outcome. You've followed the Transition Game steps. You've made *Commitments to Change* and you've had great results. Why would you detach yourself from that? Well, if your results are great, that doesn't mean that you're great. It's the same as having messy results. That doesn't make you messy. There are so many factors that affect each result. So often we tie ourselves up with the worry about getting good results instead of handling situations with the right approach.

I will never attest to know or communicate as well as Teepa Snow, a well-known dementia expert. Teepa is an occupational therapist who cares for dementia patients and teaches others to do the same. She has clinical appointments with Duke University's School of Nursing and UNC-Chapel Hill's School of Medicine.[3] When you listen to Teepa explain how to deal with dementia patients, she explains approach over outcome. I have seen her demonstrate how a dementia patient reacts to verbal input from others and how the right approach is crucial.

Instead of catching a dementia patient doing something wrong and saying, "Uh-Oh...What are they doing wrong?" we should seek the right approach and say "Aha...Now, I understand where they're coming from." Instead of correcting a dementia patient when they misunderstand you or they have told you something multiple times, Ask them to, "Tell me about it" and let them explain.

This is just an example of approach over outcome. We all don't deal with dementia patients on a regular basis like Teepa or the people she teaches, but we will all deal with situations that require us to look at approach rather than outcome. In sports, if you approach each play the best you can, you will get better results. But it's not because you focused on those results in the first place. Results are just a by-product of approach. Sure…room should be left for strategy and results are still important. In order to get to a winning strategy and produce great results, a certain approach will need to be taken, but once the approach is committed, that approach must be the focus.

Lessons Learned

You must have your own VALUES: Validation; Appraisal; Look; Utterance; Eyes; and Sense. Each of us is valuable. You don't need **validation**. God already made you valid. Always start a process by gauging what the desired results will be. This **appraisal** process will determine your success rate. We must be able to gauge results. If you don't have an appraisal process, you won't have verifiable results. Set your own sights and understand what you seek. Investigate, search, examine, and inquire to have your own **look**. After we study and look through our direction use your voice to announce your *Commitment to Change*. This **utterance** is what we use to articulate our decisions with precision and make them known. There will be no real *Commitment to Change* if you just repeat what sounds good without researching for yourself. In order to see where you're going, you must passionately own your vision by seeing it with your **eyes**. Do your own exploration and see your own evidence. Common **sense** is using all of the common faculties (sight, hearing, smell, taste, or touch) to perceive a stimulus. This stimulus is a catalyst for a *Commitment to Change*.

Something wrong (the "means") cannot be right (justified) just because the outcome (the "ends") works out. To justify something or someone is to show that something or someone is right. The ends do not justify the means. The rightness of an action is not based on the outcome. However, do not hold on to this understanding with a tight and narrow view so that you might completely disregard the end. That's not right either.

Now, detach yourself from the outcome. If your results are great, that doesn't necessarily mean that you're great. There are many factors that affect each result. So often we tie ourselves up with the worry about getting good results instead of handling situations with the right approach. Instead of catching someone doing something wrong and catching them in their wrongness, ask someone to "Tell me about it" and let them explain. There may be good lessons in their words. Results are just a by-product of approach.

Chapter 10
Milestones

Milestones

If you look at the milestones of child development and business, they're not that different. Whether the milestones include those of a growing child or a burgeoning business, each goes through the following process.

- **Gross motor**
- **Fine motor**
- **Language**
- **Cognitive**
- **Social**[4]

The **Gross motor** milestone uses a large amount of energy just to stand on two feet and keep balance. Changing positions may happen at this point, but very slowly. The next milestone called **Fine motor** occurs when we are able to use our hands to feed ourselves. These same hands can be used to play or write. The **Language** milestone happens when we find our voice as an organization or as a child. We learn how to communicate and understand what others are trying to communicate to us. We have an edge on animals with **Cognitive** thinking skills. We learn. We understand more. We problem-solve. We reason and we remember in this stage. It's silly to call humans just another animal. We were designed slightly differently. We have the ability to comprehend and contemplate. Finally, we interact with each other. Our **Social** milestone occurs when we interact with others and have relationships with family, friends, and business partners. In this stage, we cooperate and respond to the feelings of others.

We are all familiar with these five basic milestones. As parents, we find ourselves measuring a child's performance based on their milestones. Business owners act in the same way. We will each be more successful when we understand the milestones before the race begins and measure progress along the way.

Landmarks

Good surfers will establish a landmark on the beach so they can bring themselves back in line with the marker and stay surfing in their sweet spot. That landmark could be anything that's recognizable like a lifeguard tower or a set of rocks. This is especially helpful when the environment or surrounding is unfamiliar. In unfamiliar surroundings, you'll need something familiar in case anything happens. When something happens that disorients a surfer, a landmark could save their life. The landmark acts as an orienting tool so that focus can be gained and helpless drifting can be avoided.

External points of reference are indicators telling us which way to go or which way not to go. By referring to something solid or fixed, we can gain meaning out of life and business. We can gain additional information and seek guidelines so that we can get to our desired results.

Sometimes we will mistake the point of reference as a landmark though. If a surfer incorrectly establishes a set of rocks as a landmark, he or she might put themselves into a danger situation. It's good to occasionally check the landmark so you can ensure the proper *Commitment to Change* is being obtained and you're not getting yourself into some situation that will cause harm to you or those around you.

Blueprints

A blueprint is simply an outline for a plan of action. In business, it's the detail that makes up a plan. It answers the question, "Who does what by when?" In order to have a *Commitment to Change*, the actual blueprint needs to be created or changed. As a business consultant, I enter a new company with the following agenda:

- Define the team
- Define Roles & Responsibilities
- Define team values, purpose, vision, & mission
- Define team projects & "Needs Assessments"
- Answer the questions: "What was the company's original charter & what is their current charter?"
- Define team success factors
- Define barriers to the plan

- Find out what specific timing constraints the team has
- Define manual practices and strategies
- Understand resources

Determining the answers to these questions will state the meaning of the business, explain or identify the essential qualities, and set forth an outline for a plan of action. If any one of these changes dramatically, a basic blueprint adjustment may be necessary and tweaking may be needed during the process in order to get to a true *Commitment to Change*.

Barriers

When barriers prevent or hinder your action or movement from the *Status Quo* to your *Commitment to Change* and block your intended path, you must remove, go around, or go through that barrier. Here are different barriers that prevent or hinder our action or movement:

- Poor planning
- Underdeveloped skills
- Bad attitudes
- Lack of training
- Communication problems
- Interrelation issues
- Terrible programs

In my last book, *The Transition Game,* I spoke about my niece, Candace Schepperle. I golfed with Candace the same year that she won the Women's Tour event CN Canadian Open as an amateur (she has since won the event as a pro). The thing that I notice most about Candace is that she is an excellent planner. She knows exactly what she intends to do to overcome barriers and how she plans to accomplish her intentions. She is successful most of the time going around or through barriers because she plans well.

Her dad, David Schepperle, is CEO of PVC Sports and a former golf pro himself. David taught his daughter how to get around barriers well. He handles golf as he does life and business. We have had good discussions about how to hit around barriers when we're on a golf course, but the same applies to getting around barriers in personal and business life too.

David said that there may be a lot of truth that trees are 90% air until you hit one. You must take calculated risks instead of hitting through a tree willy-nilly just because you've been taught that trees are 90% air. Calculating the risk of hitting a golf ball through a tree has a lot to do with skill level, the size of the limbs and leaves, and whether there is a will to take that risk. It may be that the commitment is made to take the risk and go through the canopy of the tree. There may be visible light that causes the decision to be made to hit through. It may be that proper analysis has been done and after that analysis, the shot goes through the canopy and never touches any part of the tree. That's where risk pays off. It also could happen that the mental calculation was off slightly and the golf ball is in worse shape than it was. Contingency planning in golf and in business is important to answer the "What if" questions to assess if the risk is worth the venture.

With risk in mind, mental calculations must be made about where the golf ball will land. There must be short and long range goals. Your short range goal may be hitting completely over the tree because the barrier seemed as thick as steel. Good golfers know different trees just like business people know the different landscapes to their industry. Palm trees are obviously denser than acacia trees. You wouldn't hit through a palm tree in golf just like you wouldn't spend money you didn't have (or couldn't get) in business. If the trunk of the tree is right in front of your ball, the only logical choice would be to hit to the side. Your short-range goal (getting out from behind the trunk of the tree) is apparent. In order to get around some barriers, our aim must not be directly at the barrier. I have a natural slice to my ball because I grip the club in such a way that causes my club face to open at the point of my shot. Professional golfers like David Schepperle have taught themselves to slice or hook on demand. They understand the physics behind the reasons that natural hooks or slices happen. Even though the trunk of a tree may be directly in his path, David can aim the ball right and curve it back left or aim the ball left and curve it back right. Pros can get around an obstacle where their long range goals have not been sacrificed.

Of course, the golf ball could end up in worse shape because of poor planning. Sometimes being aggressive with a shot is counter-productive. When aggression is not required or skill level doesn't match the ability to hit a shot, it may take three or four shots to accomplish short and long range goals instead of one. This happens more often than we think. Andy Bean, with 11 PGA Tour wins, was considered an aggressive golfer. When he was asked if he ever fired at the center of the green (the safe zone), he answered that he did...when they put the pin there. He flexed to his circumstances, though, and his skill level matched his aggressive play. You don't always aim directly at the hole. Tiger Woods said Augusta National was the ultimate think-tank because everyone is constantly aiming away from the pin. You know when you're ready. When you've practiced or done it before, whether it's business or life, you take the risk and take the shot. But if you haven't done it before and the skill level is low while the risk is high, taking the shot may not be advisable. Why wouldn't you just walk into the street without looking both ways? If you do that during rush hour, you'll probably get hit. The risk is not worth the reward.

You have to want to be the best. In order to be the best, you need to work on awkward shots that you may think you could never get up and down on. But you keep working on it. Those awkward shots are just barriers. You must have the imagination AND the tenacity of a Seve Ballesteros. It may have looked like Seve Ballesteros was a very imaginative golfer, but I guarantee that he had hit many of those imaginative shots before in practice. David Schepperle can hit a golf ball and skip it across the water three out of five times. In a tournament, it may be a shot that everyone would think had never been done before, but he practiced that shot over and over again where he could make the mistake and it wouldn't cost him anything.

Wisdom is watching someone else cross a barrier and learning how to do it. People don't necessarily have to know by experience how to drive a car when they begin because they've watched it being modeled by their parent or guardian. Wise people learn how to take down or cross barriers by watching others. But the true test is when they do it themselves. There are those times that people will fall short or won't even try...but then 99.9% of the putts that are left short don't go in.

Lessons Learned

Each development in life or business goes through a milestone process of Gross motor, Fine motor, Language, Cognitive, and Social markers. The Gross motor milestone helps you stand on your own two feet and balance. Fine motor skills use our hands for intricate work. Our voice, where communication and understanding comes from, is from the Language milestone. Cognitive thinking skills help us learn, understand more, and problem-solve. We reason and we remember in this cognitive stage. And, finally, our Social milestone happens when we interact with others and have relationships. We measure performance based on each milestone. Success comes when we understand the milestones that we're in and plan beforehand what progress we'll make so we can measure it.

Landmarks provide something recognizable when the environment or surrounding area is unfamiliar. In unfamiliar surroundings where we may become disoriented a landmark acts as an orienting tool so that focus can be gained and helpless drifting can be avoided. External indicators tell us which way to go by referring to something solid or fixed. We can gain additional information and seek guidelines so that we can get to our desired results. Mistaking a reference point may cause harm to you or those around you so checking and verifying landmarks along the way is an important step.

A blueprint is an outline for a plan of action. Who does what by when? It is important to come up with a blueprint before building anything. It states the meaning, identifies the essential qualities, and sets forth an outline for a plan of action. Keep in mind that adjustments may be necessary.

Barriers like poor planning, underdeveloped skills, bad attitudes, or communication problems hinder our movement from the Status Quo to our Commitment to Change. We must remove, go around, or go through barriers. We have to know exactly what we intend to do to overcome barriers and how we plan to accomplish our intentions. There are certain calculated risks based on skill level, the size of the barrier, and the willingness to take the risk that must be accounted for. Contingency planning is important to answer the "What if" questions to assess if the risk is even worth the venture. Mental calculations must be made regarding a landing point. There must be short and long range goals adjusted for different landscapes.

We can end up in worse shape than when we started because of poor planning. Sometimes being aggressive is counter-productive when aggression doesn't match ability. You have to want to be the best. In order to be the best you must work more where you don't naturally perform well. Imagination and the tenacity to practice is crucial. Wise people also learn how to take down or cross barriers by watching others.

Chapter 11
Level Set

Level Set

Level-set is a nice corporate-sounding term bantered around in business meetings, which simply means to "get everyone on the same page" or "bring everyone up to speed." The idea is that those involved have the same basic understanding of a situation or project as everyone around them. There must be some type of alignment. There has to be some baseline of mutual understanding.

Let's talk about relationships. There are some relationships that you can look at from the outside and see that people just belong together. These people enjoy the same activities and share the same passions in life. Other relationships are not as easy to understand because the people seem so dissimilar that there is no apparent reason for the couple to be together. Some of those relationships last and some don't. The relationships that last use those dissimilarities to complement each other and draw from each other. They level-set because they understand the interdependence necessary to carry on through this life and they hold each other up. They don't hold each other down. Still, other couples that seem dissimilar won't last because instead of building each other up, they look at diversity as something to be mocked. These couples complain about the differences in their partner instead of relishing the difference. They will change or fail.

It's important to seek wise counsel before entering into a long-term relationship...and yes: marriage to a spouse is one of those long-term relationships. Marriage counseling is vital. A business partnership is another long-term relationship that must be level-set. A business plan is crucial so that the partners will complement each other and not tear each other down or the business apart. If you have individuals in a business relationship that don't level-set, it's like putting an ox and a donkey together pulling a plow. An ox and a donkey will strain against each other. They're not smart enough to look for how their differences can be used. The 4 things that oxen and donkeys don't do that would help them succeed are:

- Communicate well
- Seek to improve the relationship
- Clarify expectations
- Synergize knowledge

When we don't communicate well, seek to improve the relationship, clarify expectations, and synergize knowledge where the whole is greater than the sum of its parts, we act like oxen and donkeys thrust together. Who are you?

Alignment

An alignment is simply an adjustment to a line. You may have to make adjustments and coordinate efforts, but alignment is a state of being in agreement. There is a common vision when everyone sees where they're going and there is cooperation with a common mission and purpose.

I've seen people completely misuse alignment for their own purposes and even though they may be out of step with an organization as a whole, they have the autonomy to be a lawful evil. Those people eliminate anyone with an opposing viewpoint under the guise of alignment. Nevertheless, fully realizing why you're committing to change gives the team their purpose. Understanding where the destination brings us delivers the vision. Planning on how to get to that destination provides the mission. In order to be aligned to the team, you must be aligned to the purpose, vision, and mission of that team. Sure, the leader provides the vision, but the team determines how they will get there. If anyone is not aligned, they should not be on the team. The purpose, vision, and mission are the key factor to see if each person is aligned.

Someone can disagree but still commit and they still may be aligned. When a car is out of alignment, one of the wheels may inherently have an element that is misaligned. It may need an adjustment. The core issue may still exist and one wheel may disagree with the others, which causes the misalignment, but if that wheel submits itself to the adjustment, it is aligned.

Aligning to a common mission helps each teammate put their priorities in order and helps the team succeed. Each person may question their commitment as much as they want, but not in front of anyone but their small circle of capable advisors. For people outside their small circle of capable advisors, everything appears in agreement.

What would you give up for your commitment? Especially in a family setting each commitment doing its work builds your life-house. This life-house requires the maturity of commitments and joining commitments together in one common theme. You can't, nor should you, go through this life alone. You may see someone else as insignificant, but they may be a needed part of your life and you may need to be aligned to that person for your long-term success. In our personal anatomy, the appendix seems insignificant. In fact, it can be removed. However, recent studies have found that the appendix seems to be a harbor for friendly bacteria and it re-populates these friendly bacteria back into the intestines. This seemingly insignificant part of your body may be crucial to its success. It works the same with seemingly insignificant parts of our family or business. Without these seemingly insignificant parts, the alignment is not complete.

To become mature in your *Commitment to Change* means to pass the instruction on to others so the alignment will continue. If you're acquainted with a teaching, be a teacher of what you've learned. There must be teachers who, by constant use, have trained themselves to distinguish good commitments from bad commitments. These teachers that understand how to be aligned, support their ideas with common paradigms so that people will understand and they discount detractors of the common ideas with foundational truth. They keep themselves sharp with the people around them and keep dull people, who would dim their senses, at a distance. They share what they have because people need to be aligned to a common purpose.

Center of the Circle

Focus on the center of the circle rather than the boundary of the circle. When we are given rules, our human tendency is to question those rules and to find the furthest limits so that we can stretch the system, but still remain within its boundary. I believe rules should be investigated. I believe it creates noble character to receive rules with great eagerness and then to examine rules each and every day to see if what is said is true. Then we might use those true rules as points of reference with which we can care for ourselves and others. But focusing on the rules may be the wrong focal point.

Some rules are just foolish. A New Zealand law that was repealed, which made it illegal for cattle to mate in fields fronting public roads, was a foolish rule. A law in Saudi Arabia, making it illegal for a woman to drive a car, is a ridiculous rule. I'm sure we can all think of these rules where we say, "What were they thinking"?

But then my attorney, Solomon Cheifer, will explain that there are laws that are good and that transcend time. You really shouldn't go around murdering people. You also shouldn't steal from people. Good rules prohibit these actions. But they are still rules that focus us on the outside of the circle and drive us away from the center. Think about what happens when the rules change. If someone is snug up against the inside of the circle and the rules become narrower, that person may now be outside of the circle. Slave owners in the United States bumped up against the edge of the circle. When slavery was abolished, they suddenly were outside of the circle. If, however, they were focused on the center of the circle and didn't own slaves, they would not have realized such a drastic change in their lifestyle. Their lifestyle was not built to last. Granted, they would not have lived the high-life when they did, but it's not worth living the high-life if you're susceptible to being devastated because of your wrong-doing.

Instead, we must be focused on the center of the circle. But here's the question. How do we find the center of the circle? It's helpful to study the following picture:

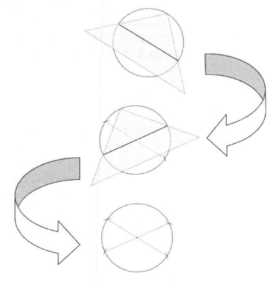

The way you find the center of the circle is to use at least two reference points that you KNOW to be true and then intersect them. In order to find the center of a real circle, you would need two triangles that you know each have a 90° corner. It doesn't matter what degrees the other corners are as long as there is that one 90° corner. Place one triangle that overlaps a circle with the 90° corner at the inside edge on any part of the curve of the circle. Mark where the sides of the right-angle cross the circle and draw a line between the two points. Repeat this process again with another right-angle triangle at different points on the circle. Where these two lines intersect is where the center of the circle is.

A good friend of mine, Mike Stefano, is a doctor and he explained to me how Thales Theorem works in real life. An x-ray is not valid unless two are taken of the same spot from different vantage points. A mass may appear to be in a patient's chest, but could actually turn out to be a shadow if a corresponding picture taken from another angle doesn't show the true image. In business, a *Commitment to Change* seldom should be taken with one piece of information. Multiple data points should also be studied so that a business knows it is following the right course. In a family, you won't find yourself going off half-cocked most of the time if you know the real story. And the real story seldom is the one to which you had a knee-jerk reaction only knowing minimal truths.

Too often, we make bad choices because we are misled or mislead ourselves by false information. The center of the circle can only be found if we have two true 90° angles. A great *Commitment to Change* can only be found with multiple true reference points. Original law would only convict a person with two or more witnesses. You could get lucky and find the center of the circle by pointing to a spot, but that's no way to live your life. It's not a good process to stumble upon good fortune. You'll wind up stumbling into a pit.

Lessons Learned

Level-setting means getting everyone on the same page and bringing everyone up to speed. It is important that everyone involved has the same basic understanding of a situation so that there is alignment and mutual understanding. Level-setting uses dissimilarities to complement and draw from others leveraging the understanding of interdependence. Counseling and planning are crucial so that partners will complement each other. If we don't communicate well, seek to improve relationships, clarify expectations, and synergize knowledge, we will ultimately fail.

An alignment is simply an adjustment to a line and the state of being in agreement where there is a common vision. Don't confuse alignment with the autonomy to do lawful evil by eliminating anyone with an opposing viewpoint though. Instead, fully realize a team's purpose and why *Commitment to Change* exists. In order to be aligned to the team, each member must be aligned to the purpose and mission of that team after the leader provides the vision. Without seemingly insignificant parts of a team, alignment is not complete and if someone is acquainted with the teaching of the team, they ought to be a teacher of what they've learned.

Rules should be investigated. It is good to receive rules and then examine them to see if what was said is true. Afterward, we can use true rules as points of reference with which we can care for ourselves and others. Unfortunately, attention to the rules is the wrong focal point. Good rules transcend time so that they don't become more narrow and people find themselves outside the rule-circle. However, we must be focused on the center of the circle. The way you find the center of the circle is to use, at least, two reference points that are known to be true and then intersect them. When you look at the same spot from different vantage points, then there is a true picture of a *Commitment to Change.*

Chapter 12
Teams

Teams vs. Groups

If you work with multiple people to accomplish a united *Commitment to Change*, make sure you work with a team rather than a group. Avoid "groupthink," which is the desire for harmony in decision-making that causes many problems when participants gloss over the examination of alternate options. Groupthink gives the illusion of harmony, but it culminates in examples like the failed hostage rescue in Iran in 1980 or the Challenger disaster in 1986 rather than beneficial examples like the Navy Seals, which is an example of precision that a team provides.

Groups tend to minimize or over-accentuate disputes. Instead, teams critically evaluate decisions in the right context. Individual rights are lost in a group because a governing body thinks it can do things better and thinks it understands how to get to the goal despite what personal doubts may be present.

I was with a company that had the over-optimistic groupthink label written all over it and the company failed because of it. A company worth over a billion dollars sold for about a hundred million because of the way they followed the design of the lackluster groups in the following table rather than the aspects of a dynamic team that is also outlined on the following page:

Teams	Groups
Are producers	Are consumers
Are assertive	Are non-threatening but pressure filled
Work toward common goals	Overuse limited techniques
Clarify Objectives	Meander
Identify hurdles in the way of their goals	Are surprised by events
Remove barriers	Are confused
Forge ahead	Are stopped
Engage	Occupy
Set up Performance Measurements to evaluate themselves	Do what's right in their own eyes
Want others to succeed and help them do it	Censor their own feelings
Are focused	Get distracted
Have long-lasting relationships	May not resolve relationship problems
Have a true sense of self	Have a false sense of invincibility
Make good decisions	Are sometimes illogical
Desire good process & results	Desire harmony
Have a great leader	Lack vision
Make great Commitment to Change	Make no commitments

I'm not suggesting that the "Groups" column is necessarily bad all the time. There may be situations that call for certain things that a group can provide. I am simply pointing out that if you desire good things that are well thought out and visionary, then be in a team and do what successful teams do instead.

A team characteristic is that each team-member doesn't have the same function as another team-member. There is one common goal, but each team-member has different skill-sets and gifts to help the team achieve that goal. These skill-sets MUST be utilized to have a productive team with the consideration of a common purpose statement that starts with "we exist to serve by…"

Each team member reports to all of the others. Some team members are teachers while others give generously of their knowledge. The leader of the team needs to be diligent in showing the way to the goal. At the same time, team members must be supportive of the leadership and not engage in destructive actions such as talking back at their desks about how awful the leader's presentation was. This just displays an unwilling march toward the goal…as if the person is grudgingly going along for the ride. Instead, team members need to have a cheerful nature with a common goal. Otherwise, they become just a group.

Teamwork happens when each team member senses a common goal and they work together to attain it. The team is more important than any one of its members alone, but each team-member must be treated equally important even if their task seems menial. I know this sounds paradoxical, but the only way for a team to function properly is that each team-member, even those that would commonly be held in low esteem, is valued while the importance of the team is established. It's one team with many parts, but the many parts form one team.

Even if someone has a bad attitude toward the team, that doesn't mean that this person ceases to be part of the team. Team members with bad attitudes need to be mentored so that they understand that not everyone will be like them. If every person were hyper-logical, where would the creativity be? If everyone paid attention to the same thing, where would the diversity of thought be? If everyone had a vision of where the team should go, where would the common purpose be? If everyone could only hear the problems, who would sniff them out, analyze them, and move them toward a solution?

Each team member has been placed in their position for a reason. Relish that!

Each team member needs the next Member. The supporting members of the team are indispensable. The members that are in the background are honorable. The leaders and salespeople don't need special treatment. There must not be any division in the Team. Disagree, but make a *Commitment to Change*! Team members must not let each other fail. If one team member looks bad, the whole team looks bad.

Partners

You can't live your life all by yourself. I know how the saying goes: "Can't" can't do anything…but let's get real. You just CAN'T live a meaningful life all by yourself!

Please don't think that it's "needy" to need other people. We weren't designed to live life alone. The following list identifies 10 steps on how to help others and have other people help you through a business or personal venture. We'll list all of the steps and then break them down one by one and work through them. In order to partner and come to the best possible result, you will need to:

1. **Identify people** that will contribute to leadership
2. Ask those identified leaders to bring others that add value (**"value-add" people**) to the process
3. **Recognize common issues** that work against preparing for the process
4. **Discover new resources** to mitigate the impact of negative issues
5. **Determine the challenge**s that the value-add people encounter so that a win-win can be produced on all levels
6. Build off the value-add **people's plans**
7. Perform **"Best Practices"** that others have created
8. **Create sustainability** by:
    (a) Continuing to do needs assessments
    (b) Continuing to goal-set
    (c) Figuring out on-going performance measurements
9. **Borrow influence** from other leaders
10. Conceive of **new ideas**

1. **Identify people that will contribute to leadership first.** Not everyone can be a leader, but you will need leaders to carry the load. When you realize everything that a leader does, you see that leadership is not a one-man show. If you sit alone at the top, it's guaranteed that other people will be standing around not doing anything. It's not good to be a solo leader. You will only wear yourself out. The work is too heavy for one person. One person cannot handle it alone. It must be understood that vision and some key decisions and direction may land on one person. One person in an organization or family must teach the others what they know, the way their subordinates or children are to be, and set a family or corporate culture and behavior. That one person also MUST select capable people around them to make judgment calls. The people that are selected must be trustworthy, hate dishonest gain, and have the faith that their actions are right. The very difficult issues are brought to the top and handled by the one leader, but every other case will be decided by these capable leaders. It will make the load lighter because it is shared partnership. Only then will one person be able to stand the strain and have goals accomplished. These simple steps I've just described are called "The Jethro Principle"[5]

2. **Ask those leaders to bring others that add value (value-add people) to the process.** With this step, you'll find that the most capable people are good at selecting capable people. You will need to go through a vetting process because mistakes will be made by capable leaders that lack maturity or miss a critical character flaw in the person they select as a value-add person. Still, this multiplication step acts exponentially to grow your business, team, or family.

3. **Recognize common issues that work against preparedness.** You'll find that once you bring leaders together, that it's easy to detect the common issues that keep them from preparing to succeed. If you keep a leader from preparing, they'll be kept from goal-setting, and if they're kept from goal-setting, there is no vision. A leader is nothing without vision. Your organization or family might as well be blind.

4. **Discover new resources to mitigate the impact of negative critical incidents.** The word "mitigate" means to moderate or lessen

in intensity. I'm not normally a fan of lessening intensity. I believe intensity is crucial to a strong Transition Game. I find that tentative progress winds up going backward. However, there are negative critical incidents that will knock an organization or family off-course. These negative critical incidents must be mitigated. The use of a Critical Incident Technique (or CIT) is especially helpful in these situations. By using this 5-step process, a negative impact can be lessened in intensity:

5–Step Critical Incident Technique (CIT)

1) Determine potential incidents
2) Fact-find and interview participants and leaders who have had similar experiences with this critical incident
3) Identify trouble
4) Make a decision on what support/new resource[s] is/are needed to resolve the trouble
5) Evaluate potential support or resource to determine if it will solve the root cause with no further problems or additional problems that are worse than the original negative critical incident.

Determine. Fact-find. Identify trouble. Make a decision on the resource. And then evaluate that support or resource to see if it will solve the root cause of the problem.

5. **Determine the challenges that the value-add people encounter so that a win-win can be produced.** Take care of your staff and family and they'll take care of you. However, do not take care of your staff and family so THAT they will take care of you. That's selfish and you're really only taking care of yourself in that situation. Serve others. Understand what it takes for the value-add people to win and help them win. Value-add people will understand what you're doing and add even more value. Win-win produces this synergy that builds on itself.

Be careful in this step. You may find yourself judging others to size them up to see if they are value-add. If they are contributing, they are value-add until they prove themselves otherwise. Don't start excluding people from the group because you, out of your own devices, have found a person to be of lessened value.

6. **Build off the value-add people's plans.** Now that the challenges that the value-add people encounter have been determined, their goals and plans should become more clear. When a leader helps remove roadblocks and barriers to help another person win, the leader can see what's behind the barrier or roadblock. When you knock down an unnecessary wall that's blocking your progress to a wild fruit tree, you see other fruit that's free for the taking.

Helping someone else win can sometimes become a huge windfall. The worst thing that can be done is to ignore the bounty that's produced after the removal of roadblocks and barriers. That's the time for action. People in sports hurt themselves when they're tentative. If the eyes can see something that is purely ethical to obtain, seize the moment and obtain it. That's the bonus that comes about by building off the plans of the value-add people. Don't ignore this step. There is great synergy in it.

7. **Copy, conclude, and carry out Best Practices.** What we find is that there are other organizations that might be facing the same challenges and going in the same direction. What we also find is that each of the successful organizations or families each developed tactics and strategies to get them from point A to point B in the most expeditious way possible. Those tactics and strategies should be duplicated. We must arrive at conclusions to ensure that those Best Practices actually fit in our environment and then if they do, carry them out to completion in our own organization or family so that we will find success through its practices.

8. **Continue needs assessments and goal-setting while figuring out on-going performance measurements. This will create sustainability.** In Jim Collins' bestselling book, "Good to Great"[6], he describes the flywheel as the victory of steadfast discipline over the quick fix. Organizations and families that desire to do the right things to make themselves successful, which include finding out: what they need to be successful (needs assessment);

how to get to that success (goal-setting); and then how to determine that they obtained success (performance measurements), will create sustainability by continuing these on-going actions. If each organization or family steadfastly applies basic life-giving principles, they will find victory even in the midst of apparent defeat.

9. **Borrow influence from other leaders.** I probably could have found a better example, but borrowed influence makes me think about Ford's use of a letter written by Bonnie & Clyde that purportedly said if they were going to steal a car, they would make it a Ford. Ford would allegedly read this letter as borrowed influence to show the value of their cars. Many pictures were taken of Bonnie & Clyde in front of their 1932 Ford V-8 B-400, which would support that letter. Be careful of this step, though. You can only go so far by borrowing someone else's influence. If influence has been borrowed and the original influencer apparently withdraws himself or herself, you'll be in worse shape than you would have been without that help in the first place.

Still, borrowed influence can help break down barriers and open doors. And if you buy into what the original influencer has to say, the influence becomes yours and people will involve themselves and buy in to what you have to say.

10. **Conceive new ideas.** After following these Partnership steps, continue to conceive new ideas. You and your team can invent new ideas. You'll become idea builders. Don't confine your ideas to your own mind. Let those ideas out. Have separate meetings just for idea processing and conception. These meetings become a bonding experience where partners will procreate, protect, and find pleasure in new ideas that are found. People establish what they conceive.

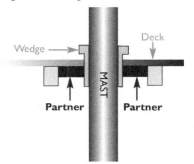

It's interesting that in sailing, a partner or a mast partner are the pieces of lumber positioned between the beams directly under the deck and right next to the opening in the ship for the mast that holds the sail. The partner supports the mast, solidifies the position of the mast, and reinforces the mast so that it won't damage itself by constantly changing direction. Partnership is crucial to sailing and it's central to a family or organization. Partners must exist to support and to solidify an organization's or family's position. They must also exist to reinforce that organization or family so that it won't be damaged by constant changing direction.

Lessons Learned

Teams are better than groups. "Groupthink" causes the desire for harmony in decision-making to gloss over the examination of alternate options. It gives the illusion of harmony, but it culminates in failure. Groups minimize or over-accentuate disputes and lose individual rights. If you desire good things that are well thought out and visionary, be in a team and do what successful teams do.

Teamwork means that each team member has different functions and there is one common goal. Skill-sets are utilized to be productive and each team member reports to all the others not grudgingly or out of compulsion. Each team member senses the common goal and they work together to attain it. The team is more important than any one of its members alone. Each team member has been placed in their position for a reason and the supporting members of the team are indispensable.

You can't do this life all by yourself. It's not "needy" to need other people. We weren't designed to go it alone. You can help others and have others help you by: asking other leaders to bring people that add value (value-add people) to the process; recognizing common issue; discovering new resources; determining the challenges that the value-add people encounter; building off the value-add people's plans; performing Best Practices; creating sustainability; borrowing influence; and conceiving new ideas.

Not everyone can be a leader, but you will need other leaders to carry the load. One person cannot handle it alone. The most capable people are good at selecting capable people. Once you bring leaders together, it's easy to detect the common issues that keep them from preparing. If you keep a leader from preparing, they'll be kept from goal-setting, and if they're kept from goal-setting, there is no vision. A leader is nothing without vision.

The word "mitigate" means to moderate or lessen in intensity. Intensity is crucial to a strong Transition Game, but negative critical incidents must be mitigated. Serve others. Understand what it takes for the value-add people to win and help them win. Don't exclude people because you have found a person to be of lessened value. Helping someone else win can sometimes become a huge windfall and there is great synergy. Certain tactics and strategies should be copied. There must be conclusions to ensure that Best Practices actually fit in an environment and then, if they do, carried out to completion. Organizations and families that desire to do the right things to be successful will create sustainability by continuing these on-going actions. Borrowed influence can help break down barriers and open doors. Become idea builders. Don't confine ideas. People establish what they conceive. Partners must exist to support and solidify an organization's or family's position. They also exist to reinforce an organization or family so it won't be damaged by changing direction.

Chapter 13
Act

Act

I have written about my cousin, David Schepperle, before. He is the CEO of PVC Sports and he explains the OODA loop without really even knowing the acronym. If you remember in my first book, *The Transition Game*, the A in OODA means Act.

US Air Force Colonel John Boyd created the OODA Loop, which stands for:

Observe
Orient
Decide
Act

If you create patterns of Observe, Orient, Decide, and then Act, you can gain a competitive advantage in business and sports when you process this loop quickly. The last step is vital to success.

You can do anything you want as long as you commit to it and take the consequences that go along with it. David Schepperle explains the OODA Loop with these steps:

1. Look at something
2. Argue both sides
3. Make a decision
4. Go all in
5. Accept the results

The best-selling product at PVC Sports is the mirror. Interestingly, the mirror gives golfers immediate feedback on their swings and people can self-monitor. Actions can be private at first, but it's hard to lie to a mirror. It is an easy formula to be negative or positive with our actions, but our job is to understand that formula.

David constantly makes his products better. He will tell you that if you follow his steps to a "T," you will improve. Only then can you alter his process to make it better. He often quotes Dennis Miller, "...of course, that's just my opinion. I could be wrong." He's not opposed to finding a better way to make a product, but the only way you can know that it's a better way, is to understand his original formula first. Then you can ask the questions, "What was my plan and what exactly happened that made it different from the original?" If the difference is important to making a better product, then it's not a good thing if the adjustment to the formula remains unmade. Of course, that's just my opinion. I could be wrong.

We should constantly ask, "Can we do it better?" I want to get into such a pattern that anything that keeps me from my *Commitment to Change* is distasteful and I ask, "can we do it better?" even if the *Status Quo* doesn't cause me pain and I like it. Sometimes, we just have to do what makes us uncomfortable. Take the path less travelled. Stay on the straight and narrow. Salt can lose its saltiness when diluted rather than have that tight Sodium and Chlorine bond. Salt-of-the-earth people are very opinionated. When they become diluted by life, they lose their opinion. Conversely, Salt-of-the-earth people may become so opinionated that they are diluted by their own opinions.

When you venture out on a new action, stay connected to your source of growth. If you remain with that source of growth, but still venture out, you will be very productive and effective. If you remove yourself from that source, you won't be able to do anything. It's like a light that is unplugged. No energy can get to it and it's useless. You might as well throw it away if it's never going to be plugged in. It's better fuel for a fire than a useless lamp. However, if you stay plugged in, you'll be unstoppable.

Act as if your *Commitment to Change* was plastered all over the newspaper tomorrow. If you were confronted with your commitment, would you claim it?

What You Have the Right to do May Not be Beneficial

You may have the right to do something, but it may not wind up being beneficial for you. Consider a partner looking after their own welfare and not taking into account the other person. Certainly, someone has the right to only look after themselves. Looking after one's self is not beneficial for a relationship, though. Every action in a relationship needs to be weighed in the light of its effect upon the other partner in the business or personal relationship. The purely selfish person will get by for a while, but selfish acts, although they are perfectly within someone's rights to do are not beneficial for long-term relationships. And that's the most important thing in this life.

I am perfectly within my rights to overeat, but my overall health would suffer. I am perfectly within my rights to drink alcohol in front of an alcoholic, but if it causes him to drink and stumble because he respects me, what have I done? A tourist could legally participate in prostitution in parts of this world, but the physical and mental disease that he would bring home to his family would last a lifetime.

There are plenty of things that could legally be done and I agree with pushing the limits, but every *Commitment to Change* must be weighed in the light of its effect on the decision maker in addition to the people around them. If you think for one moment that you are perfectly within your rights to do something that is ultimately not beneficial for you, you are mastered by it.

Those that live by a nature that says, "I have the right!" have their minds set on what those rights desire. However, those who live in accordance with their *Commitment to Change*, a good and right change, have their minds set on what is good and right. I can't go on enough about fixing our eyes on the right kind of change. It bears repeating that "great" can be defined in two ways. The first definition of great, "of extraordinary quality, ability, or distinction," is what we want. The second definition of great, "Exceptional in degree or intensity," is only desirable if it's been preceded by the first definition. As I pointed out in my last book, you can have huge, sweeping, volcano-sized change that could be described as great, but destroys everything in its path. You can also have huge, sweeping, volcano sized rights, but they may not be beneficial for you.

Strategy

Strategy is just prioritizing tactical decisions. The dictionary describes strategy as "a plan, method, or series of maneuvers…for obtaining a specific goal or result." Those maneuvers are the tactics. I know it sounds like a paradox, but good habits should be built with tactics first…good or bad.

I haven't met anyone that can be trusted as a strategist who didn't spend time being trusted with tactics. Someone who is bad at tactics will also be bad at strategy unless they get lucky. In order to develop a strategic mind-set so that you can obtain a specific goal or result, a method or series of maneuvers must be accomplished.

This is where it sounds a little contradictory, though. You've heard me say it before. You've seen me write that, "The ends do NOT justify the means." Some people understand that to mean that there should be no bad tactics. That is the furthest reasoning from the truth. Poor tactics will occur. We live in a fallen world. Negative tactics are everywhere…and while you wouldn't purposely create bad tactics, you can use them to your benefit.

At some point, we'll be asked to give an account of our management of tactics. Act shrewdly in business before you do. Unfortunately, the same people that will understand the concepts in this book are the same people that may not completely buy-in to turning around negative tactics to their benefit. People that act shrewdly as a natural course of business and create bad tactics as a habit are better at using those bad tactics to their benefit. Make it your practice to turn lemons into lemonade. If you're faithful transitioning even the most minute bad tactics to good strategy, you'll be faithful creating a great strategy. Be careful though. If you focus on bad tactics and make that a habit in business or your personal life, you won't consistently create a great strategy. You can't have both. You'll wind up hating a good strategy if you love dirty money. A good heart will tell the difference.

Reserves

When something is held in reserve, it's set apart for a particular purpose. In business, a reserve could be a liquid asset (easily converted to cash) available in case of emergency or a portion of the company profits that are not distributed. With a family, a reserve could be an earthquake kit that has an accumulation of food and survival goods. In life, it could be acting with reservations about a certain person because of lack of trust. All of these examples of reserves avoid one suggestion: These examples avoid the suggestion that "reserves" are to be used first. Reserves are meant exactly for what their name suggests. These examples indicate something to be set aside for a particular probable or possible purpose.

Misconceptions remain in this world. Even the Federal Reserve is a deceptive name. The name "Federal Reserve" covers up that they are privately owned and do not carry reserves. The Federal Reserve actually creates money and loans it to the US government in exchange for U.S. bonds. The United States' debt is endless because it is monetized. Still with the misconceptions and deceptions commonly held, there are people that will see through it and make corrections. Presidents Jackson and Lincoln eliminated the debt by doing things like withdrawing funds from the central bank and having Congress print full legal tender. This eliminated the control and stopped replacing Plan A with Plan B.

Don't make your plan B your plan A unless your Plan A fails. Your Plan B is meant to function as a reserve and used only if you need it. Plan B is not meant to act as a distraction to Plan A. Reserves can act as a diversion to the intentional and deliberate process it takes to make Plan A succeed. Don't let that happen.

Lessons Learned

The OODA Loop stands for Observe, Orient, Decide, and Act. If you create patterns of Observe, Orient, Decide, and then Act, you can gain a competitive advantage in business and sports when you process this loop quickly. The final step, "Act," is vital to success. Follow action steps exactly and then alter the process to make it better. Then you can ask the questions, "What was my plan and what exactly happened that made it different from the original?" If the difference is important enough to make or achieve a better product or service, then make the adjustment. No matter what the situation is, we should constantly ask, "Can we do it better?"

When you venture out on a new action, stay connected to your source of growth. If you remain with that source of growth and venture out, you will be productive and effective. If you remove yourself from that source, you won't be able to achieve anything. Act as if you're Commitment to Change was plastered all over the newspaper tomorrow.

You may have the right to do something, but it may not wind up being beneficial for you. Every action in a relationship needs to be weighed in the light of its effect upon the other partner in the business or personal relationship. There are plenty of things that can be legally done and in some cases I agree with pushing the limits, but every *Commitment to Change* must be weighed in the light of its effect on the decision maker in addition to the people around them. Those that live by a nature that says, "I have the right!"

have their minds set on what those rights desire, but those who live in accordance with their *Commitment to Change*, a good and right change, have their minds set on what is good and right.

Strategy is just prioritizing tactical decisions. The dictionary describes strategy as "a plan, method, or series of maneuvers...for obtaining a specific goal or result." Those maneuvers are the tactics. When I say, "The ends do NOT justify the means," some people understand that to mean that there should be no negative tactics. While you wouldn't purposely create poor tactics, you can use negative tactics to your benefit.

When something is held in reserve, it's set apart for a particular purpose. Reserves are not meant to be used first. Reserves are meant to indicate something to be set aside for a particular probable or possible purpose. Don't make your plan B your plan A unless your Plan A fails. Your Plan B is meant to be kept in reserve and used if you need it. Plan B is not meant to act as a distraction to Plan A. Reserves can act as a diversion to the intentional and deliberate process it takes to make Plan A succeed.

THE FOURTH C:
Character

Chapter 14
Genuine Article

The Genuine Article

The genuine article is not some cheaply made substitute. Counterfeiters get a free ride sometimes. Counterfeits are made in imitation so that they can be passed off as the genuine article. That's deceptive. That's a forgery. And it works for a period of time…but not forever. Because counterfeiters don't possess the acclaimed or attributed character of the genuine article, they will not pass off as authentic or realistic in the long run. Because counterfeiters do not enjoy the quality or the origin of the genuine article, they will not have the deep care for people and results and they definitely will NOT inspire confidence.

You'll have to trust me on this because it does appear that the people that cheat get the best of everything. Just know that it isn't true that counterfeiters get the best of everything. They don't get to experience care, true love, and confidence. Counterfeiters don't get to experience being the genuine article and being the genuine article, in and of itself, is the best of everything.

Transparency

For our purposes, transparency is used to describe a behavior of being clear and letting the light be shined on a situation…even if it may be embarrassing. Transparent people, fortunately or unfortunately, show their warts. Transparency depicts someone who is open and accountable.

Mark Zuckerberg, co-creator of Facebook, said "By giving people the power to share, we're making the world more transparent." Remarkably, many Human Resource departments now covertly research Facebook and other social networking sites to investigate their potential hires. Many people have not been hired because of the life they reveal or the blemishes they show to their friends that others also see. Unfortunately, the life and blemishes may be distorted to the people viewing the information. Social media may unintentionally follow Snell's law. Snell's law allows light to be bent at a negative angle of refraction as it passes through a seemingly transparent interface. Nature's example happens when a ray of sunlight is bent when it passes through the surface of the water. A business example of Snell's law happens when the observation of a person's life is obscured by the picture painted on social media.

The "full disclosure" principle states that the information that is disclosed considers the events that have material impact on an entity's financial position. There is just too much information in a normal business to share every nitty-gritty detail. A business shouldn't share every facet of their company and thus give away their competitive advantage. That would just be foolish. There are certain trade secrets and inner-dealings that should be shared internally with wise counsel only.

People should act the same way in their personal lives. Be clear, let the light shine on even the circumstances that can be embarrassing, but share potentially harmful information only with wise counsel.

Water Seeks Its Own Level

Water is fluid and liquid finds its own constancy. Water finds out where it fits no matter what the container looks like. Water that is united in some way to another container will find the level of the other container and match it. If you have a "U" shaped pipe filled with water, you'll see that the water on one side of the pipe will be at the same level as the water on the

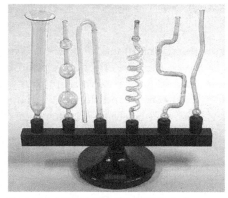

Device for demonstrating that water seeks its own level, no matter the size or shape of the container. (http://museum.nbta.ca/science_artefacts.htm)

other side of the pipe. No matter how you tilt your cup, one side of the water line in your cup will match the other side of the water line. That's just how things physically occur...unless, of course, you have some outside force acting upon the liquid to keep it from appearing at the same level.

I grew up with a group of guys that always hung around together and spurred each other on. We always encouraged each other and were there for each other. We also did completely idiotic stuff together that created some long-term damage. Despite this, we all obtained our Bachelor's degrees and some of us went on to acquire more advanced degrees and certifications. "The Boys" are now all hard-working men and all of us have demonstrated a capacity to love someone else wholeheartedly. When we have an opportunity to meet up after a long absence, my heart is glad and we act like we have never been apart. Years ago, I remember one of the mothers of one of the boys approaching a couple of us and thanking us, "because," she said, "my son never would have gotten his degree if you boys weren't in his life."

Fortunately, I grew up with a group of guys that had goals and plans for life. They were all driven individuals that knew how to have fun. We all had our own personalities. Jason was the teacher. Lyle was headstrong. David was the fun-loving one. Jeff was more cerebral than any of us and was usually right about most things. I was called "Mongo" because I was more intense than everyone else. But we were all a tight group because we were all driven leaders that could see a plan's results before they happened. Politically and theologically, we are as diverse as can be. But we all enjoy that diversity because it becomes synergy that adds to our group's water level.

I previously mentioned actions that hurt us in the long-term. Those actions can have a negative effect on relationships and decrease our all-over water level. Outside forces can disrupt your water level. Sometimes events in your life will affect you and clog that U shaped pipe. Your water will seek its own level, but may be stopped by negative change agents such as:

1. Unhealthy life-style of you or a loved-one
2. Unresolved marital tension
3. Illegal activity
4. Careless physical activity
5. A bad economy

If your only job implementing a new strategy or plan is to remove a barrier so that the level of those involved can be at a certain point above where you are, that implementation is far easier. The complications start when water seeks its own level at a lower point than where it currently resides.

A book by Jim Collins called "How the Mighty Fall"[7] states that you can't change culture. You won't be able to change your organization's culture unless you change the mindset (level) of staff that you have. Seldom is a family's culture changed unless there is an outside force adding value (water) to the relationship. The level of newcomers with the right culture will affect change in positive ways and will cause the level of the overall organization's culture to rise. If the culture of any individual does not match the organization's culture, they will conform or remove themselves.

Lessons Learned

The genuine article acts as a leader of a Commitment to Change. The genuine article cares deeply and inspires confidence. Counterfeiters are deceptive and they may work for a period of time…but not forever because they don't possess the acclaimed or attributed character of the genuine article. Just because it appears that people who cheat get the best of everything doesn't make it so. They never get to experience care, true love, and confidence.

Transparency is used to describe a behavior of being clear and letting the light be shined on a situation that, in some circumstances, may be embarrassing. Transparency depicts someone who is open and accountable…not like Snell's Law that allows light to be bent at a negative angle of refraction as it passes through a seemingly transparent interface. People should act clearly and let the light shine on the circumstances that can even be embarrassing.

Water, just like a person, finds out where it fits no matter what the shape of container. No matter how you tilt your life, one side of your life will match the other side. Unless there is some outside force, duplicity doesn't last forever. Don't confuse duplicity with diversity, though, because diversity becomes synergy that adds to our water level.

Sometimes our only job is to remove a barrier so that the level of those involved can be at a certain point above where they began. The complications start when water seeks its own level at a lower point than where it started. You won't be able to change your organization's culture unless you change the mindset (level) or staff that you have.

Chapter 15
All for Show

It's All for Show

About 40 billionaires got together in 2010 and decided to give away half of their wealth before they died. Although the idea seemed to have been an act of philanthropy, the billionaires made a show of it and their charitable acts became a public spectacle. Charity shouldn't come with a parade. Even if they gave away half their wealth to make a point for others to follow, that in and of itself doesn't define philanthropy. One of the donors said he only contributed because another well-known billionaire (that started this donor drive) told him to do it. Philanthropy comes from two words that the Greeks put together: *Philos* meaning "loving and caring for" while ánthropos means a "human being."

Loving and caring for another human being may be disconnected from making a point about loving and caring for another human being. Loving and caring for another human being is also disconnected from taking that action just because somebody else told you to do it. Interestingly, the "y" at the end of the word philanthropy is an English suffix which completes the word by saying that the person taking this action is inclined to or characterized by it. Essentially the whole word philanthropy is the action characterized by someone loving other human beings. A Philanthropist is a lover of other people. His or her actions are guided and controlled by love. A Philanthropist's heart should be right, good, and pure.

In 2011, a video went viral of a teacher in Mexico that sang to her students while gunfire rang outside. Martha Rivera Alanis kept her students unruffled and safe by talking calmly to them and refocusing the children's minds on something other than the bullets that could kill them. She kept them on the floor where the bullets could not find them. Her students were kept safe. At one point in the video, she said to one worried child, "No, my love, nothing is going to happen, just put your little face on the floor." That day, Martha Rivera Alanis took action that was characterized by love for her children.

Sacrifice of Fools

A "Sacrifice of Fools" happens when there are a lot of words and empty promises from someone who doesn't even know what they're saying or doing wrong.

I know someone who would play the "Yes is No" game with their children because they thought it was fun. They found it odd that I wouldn't play along and they thought, since I was the outsider, that there must be something wrong with me. Nevertheless, it is fundamentally wrong to teach that "Yes" means "No."

This "Yes is No" game seems like an extreme example, yet how many times have we seen a politician make a collection of promises only to find that once they get into political office, those same promises are not kept? Or how many times have there been backroom deals that contradict what the politician said in public?

It's interesting that playing politics can be defined as *the use of strategy in obtaining power or control* or it can be defined as *dealing with people in an opportunistic, manipulative, or devious way.* "Playing politics" sounds like using the "Yes is No" game for a power-grab. This power-grab happens regardless of cost to the same people the manipulators are claiming to help. Anyone who loves playing politics uses an abundance of words to make empty promises and they don't even know they're doing anything wrong. Playing politics is a sacrifice of fools.

Strain at a Gnat

"Strain at a gnat" is an idiom that signifies much solicitude (those things that cause anxiety) about little things and none about greater things. Think about taking a gnat out of your drink. Wouldn't most of us just throw the drink out because of the many germs that were left behind by the gnat itself? Think about how disgusting the residue is that's left behind even if you do throw it out. Many people, however, salvage objects in their lives. These objects have a residue that damages lives and causes pain. But the residue is sight unseen and if we can't see it, we think it must not be there. What we don't see often times, however, may kill us.

If you were hungry enough, I'm sure a camel could be eaten. I don't ever plan to eat a camel myself because many consider camels unclean animals that spit. Nevertheless, many people in this world do eat camel. The flesh itself is not unpalatable even though it's dry and tough. I hear that everything from the camel's hump to the tongue can be chewed and digested by a human. The hump can even be dissolved to make tea. I mention this because it is possible to eat a camel and it is possible to strain a gnat out of your drink. However, you can never be sure you've strained all the germs out of your drink. Also, I hear that the after-taste of a camel is absolutely horrible.

Regardless of the path of displeasure that you take, the metaphor that is being created here is that while neither is a good choice, both are not necessarily good practices. Discard the drink rather than digest the germs and don't purposely eat something that you know has bad flavor and leaves a bad after-taste. Especially, don't spend a lot of time on little things when the damage left behind is what does the real harm especially while you unthinkingly do something so repulsive that drives the right relationships away.

I had a conversation with someone close to me about the first day of autumn. I insisted that a certain day was the beginning of autumn. I later thought about why I would cause something so simple to be of such concern to me. Why would I even say anything? On top of everything, this person was right and I was wrong. Regardless of right or wrong in this situation, I was straining at a gnat but swallowing a camel. I was expressing excessive attentiveness to a meaningless argument when the damage that the disagreement left behind caused the real harm. This disagreement was so repulsive that a right relationship was driven away for a time.

Straining at a gnat happens whenever we say, "The other person was also wrong." Does that make it right for you to do? Two wrongs don't make a right. There are also many people in this world that suffer from Obsessive Compulsive Disorder (OCD) who strain at gnats. People with OCD aim to reduce their anxiety by performing ritualistic exercises repetitiously. They have become superstitious and they believe that their actions influence the reward.[6] If you're thinking that you're not OCD and this doesn't apply to you, think about:

- Being fixated on something
- Being a perfectionist
- Hoarding things
- Being absorbed in a cause for the wrong reason
- Believing in chance or magic
- Holding onto beliefs that are not productive because "that's the way we've always done it."

This list of traits strains at gnats but swallows camels.

Lessons Learned

Charity shouldn't come with a parade. Philanthropy comes from two words put together: *Philos* meaning "loving and caring for" while ánthropos means a "human being." The "y" at the end of the word philanthropy is an English suffix which completes the word by saying that the person taking the action is inclined to or characterized by it. Philanthropy is the action characterized by someone loving other human beings. A Philanthropist is a lover of other people. A Philanthropist's heart is right, good, and pure.

A "Sacrifice of Fools" happens when there are a lot of words and empty promises from someone who doesn't know what they're talking about. Promises that were not kept contradict what was said in public. Playing politics can be defined as *"the use of strategy in obtaining power or control"* or *"dealing with people in an opportunistic, manipulative, or devious way."*

The term "strain at a gnat" is an idiom that signifies causing anxiety about little things with no concern about greater things. Some objects of our attention have a residue that damages our lives and causes pain. What we don't see may kill us. Regardless of right or wrong, expressing excessive attentiveness to a meaningless argument causes real harm by the damage that the disagreement leaves behind. Straining at a gnat happens whenever we say, "The other person was wrong also." Two wrongs do not make a right.

Chapter 16
Integrity

Integrity

Integrity is defined as MAKING and keeping commitments. Too often people will not make commitments at all just so they appear virtuous when they don't break the commitments that they never made. Integrity is the adherence to those MADE commitments concerning certain principles. Integrity makes you whole. If you are a person of integrity, you walk your talk in perfect condition…not because you did your work perfectly, but because you approached your work with a perfect mindset…a mindset of integrity.

When I look back on my life, I want to be weighed and evaluated with an honest scale and found with integrity. I know that I won't have done everything right and I know the failings I must compensate for. However, the integrity that I've found is that I stuck with the program, avoided the "get rich quick" schemes, and followed the narrow path. Neither should I allege the example of the many as an excuse for doing wrong. Believe me when I say, I've made almost every mistake in the book…some intentionally and some unintentionally. I've been carried away with every imaginable thought that is evil to man. I was a bad man and I know the difference between integrity and deceit. I can explain to others because I have failed. I've had my helping of emptiness.

Dignity is different than integrity, though. Integrity has to do with character and dignity is the elevation of that character. My dignity means nothing without my integrity. There are a lot of attributes that mean nothing without integrity. Warren Buffet said that "In looking for people to hire, you look for three qualities: integrity, intelligence, and energy. And if they don't have the first, the other two will kill you."

Quite frankly, it's better to be poor with your integrity than a fool who doesn't know which end is up. As Abraham Lincoln said, "Nearly all men can stand adversity, but if you want to test a man's character, give him power." There are some powerful fools in this world. Sure…power is just the rate at which energy is transferred, but if power is transferred to someone who doesn't have integrity, a lethal prescription will ensue.

Justice

Justice is the quality of conforming to a principle. People who are principle-centered are mature and productive. The late Stephen Covey in his book "Principle-Centered Leadership" says "to value oneself and, at the same time subordinate oneself to higher purposes and principles is the paradoxical essence of highest humanity and the foundation of effective leadership" [8].

Being just, equitable, and true allows our actions to be grounded with reason and determines our conduct. People who do justice are courageous, treat others with respect, and deal with situations in a relational rather than a transactional way. Unfortunately, we all deal with people, including ourselves at times, who are self-righteous. They find it their job to administer punishment to others and show favoritism with their rewards. They are the legally minded, but not in a way that a good attorney like mine practices law. These people become judge, jury, and executioner to the people that need kindness and mercy the most. They are not humble and their ways are often distorted. These are the people from whom we need to steer clear. We must not steer clear from them in a judgmental way, though, lest we fall into the same trap of becoming self-righteous ourselves.

Our goal is to pursue justice, and only justice that we would live in peace and stay in that sweet spot where we never have too much or too little. A good friend of mine, Ned Webster, who is the CEO and President of NLW Concrete pursues justice in the right way. He is a principle-centered leader who subordinates himself to higher purposes. He is just, he seeks kindness and mercy, and he walks humbly. Sure, he's just a man, but I would rather be just a man and be like Ned than to own the whole world and lose my soul. The reason that Ned's company is successful (and his father before him and his son's will be after him) is because he is just. He exemplifies justice.

Shrewd but Innocent

There is peacefulness that comes along with being innocent, but that innocence is not naivety. Peacefulness does not mean that someone is not astute or sharp with practical matters. Quite the opposite, there is innocent peacefulness when we have a grasp of reality. People do not trust naivety, cunning, or unethical behavior. However, they do trust someone who is truly innocent, but knows what they're doing.

Sometimes, you need to navigate through a hostile workplace. Navigation is hard in these circumstances, but it's harder if we don't know what we're doing or if we are restless about what is going on around us. Innocence is simplicity…freedom from complexity. Essentially, you know what you're doing and you make it easy for others to know what they're doing.

There is light shed on this subject when we think about where shrewdness and innocence come from. When we are astute and sharp, it is our minds. When we are innocent, it is our hearts. Regrettably, many people have mistaken innocence as passivity and they take a passive approach to life. Those people don't attain their goals. Still others mistake shrewdness as cunning. There is a difference between being sly or deceiving about something and being sharp about practical matters. You must understand what might slip you up and what could cause you harm so that you can navigate around problems. You must know your enemy and yourself. Chinese general Sun Tzu who lived 500 B.C. said:

"If you know your enemy and you know yourself, you need not fear the result of a hundred battles."

This sentence covers two aspects of human behavior: The awareness of shrewdness and the fearlessness of innocence. I wouldn't exactly call Sun Tzu innocent because he was a Chinese military general skilled in war. Nevertheless, the points in his book, "The Art of War"[9], are clear about winning and managing conflict with guiltlessness. It turns out that if you're guiltless, you're innocent so, just maybe, Sun Tzu was shrewd AND innocent.

Lessons Learned

Integrity is making and keeping commitments. Integrity is the adherence to commitments concerning certain principles. Integrity makes you whole. If you are a person of integrity, you walk your talk in perfect condition. Dignity is different than integrity. Integrity has to do with character and dignity is the elevation of that character. Dignity means nothing without integrity. It's better to be poor with your integrity than a fool who doesn't know which end is up. If power is transferred to someone who doesn't have integrity, a lethal prescription will ensue.

Justice is the quality of conforming to a principle. People who are principle-centered are mature and productive. Being just, equitable, and true allows our actions to be grounded with reason and it determines our conduct. The goal is to pursue justice. A principle-centered leader will subordinate himself or herself to higher purposes. He or she is just, they seek kindness and mercy, and walk humbly.

There is peacefulness that comes along with being innocent, but that innocence is not naivety. Peacefulness does not mean that someone is not astute or sharp with practical matters. Quite the opposite, there is innocent peacefulness when we have a grasp of reality. Innocence is simplicity, which is freedom from complexity. Astuteness and sharpness come from our minds. Innocence comes from our hearts. Many people have mistaken innocence as passivity. Others mistake shrewdness as cunning. There is a difference. Manage conflict with guiltlessness. It turns out that if you're guiltless, you're innocent.

THE FOURTH C Character

Chapter 17
Endurance & Stamina

Endurance & Stamina

Your *Commitment to Change* is an endurance race not a sprint. I ran the 880 (800 Meter) race in High School, which was a unique race because a runner really needs to run it with a time dramatically under 2 minutes in order to be competitive. This makes this half-mile race an endurance race at a sprint pace. That means that you will need a lung capacity that will allow you to start out strong while conserving enough energy to keep going until the end. You keep your lung capacity strong by standing straight up with only a slight lean forward. You'll stay up on the balls of your feet just like you would during a sprint and balance it off with a lean. That creates energy efficiencies. During the 800 Meter race, a runner must start and finish strong. The same thing happens in business. You need a strong start AND you need to reach your goals with vigor.

You can only have a strong start AND reach your goals vigorously if you build endurance for the long haul, though. *Commitment to Change* is an endurance race not a sprint and it takes practice. You won't be able to break any world records without a lot of it. When I was younger, I had shin splints in both legs. I got shin splints because I hated practice. I hated the drills. I hated having to perform when nobody was watching. I did love to run, but I wasn't balanced about it. I would run for long periods in a dry concrete river bed, which only contributed to my pain. I remember near the end of my shin splint injury. There was a race that didn't have runners because of injury or absence so I knew that if I ran through the pain, I would place. I was never inactivated so I entered the race while the coach was at a field event and he couldn't stop me. I still remember the gun going off and starting that race. The pain that immediately shot through my legs was tremendous. I can still see in my mind the coach running toward me as I started limping. He was screaming at me to stop so that I wouldn't injure myself further and be out for the whole season. But I knew that if, at least I finished, I would score points for the team. I ran through the pain that day and finished. I had a very angry coach, but I knew I could score so I kept going. I recovered quicker than expected after that. I would regularly throw up before races because of butterflies in my stomach, but as long as my legs felt good, I was ready to race.

Nevertheless, endurance and stamina have more to do with a balanced approach. Endurance and stamina both take practice. We have hope because of the encouragement that endurance provides and we have more endurance because we are inspired by hope. It is an attitude of mind and it acts on itself so that we can persevere even though we are persecuted or going through trials. However, it is not to your credit if you do something wrong and endure it. The hope, encouragement, inspiration, and perseverance from endurance and stamina come from doing good and suffering for it. Not doing poorly and suffering for it.

"All's Well That Ends Well" vs. Machiavelli (The Prince)

To be Machiavellian means to be manipulative for dishonest gain and to be self-serving. Machiavelli wrote to certain princes in the early 1500's that those "who have accomplished the most have been accomplished at deception" and that they "must be a good liar." Machiavelli was an "Ends Justifies the Means" kind of guy. A large population still subscribe to this mindset. I talked about Shakespeare in my last book, *The Transition Game*[2], and said that you can get past problems as long as the end is good. You can put up with the not-so-fun-in-between-transitional times if you know the ending will be better.

No wonder Machiavellianism was considered a plague in the 16th century culminating in up to tens of thousands of deaths. Today, a Machiavellian is that sociopath that has that grandiose view of himself or herself. They don't have the capacity to love so they lack the empathy to relate to the pain of others. They replace that lack of empathy with utter contempt for any kind of suffering…to the point of taking advantage of that suffering for their personal gain.

Machiavellians don't think anything is wrong with their cunning lifestyle and they can readily justify their crimes against other people without any trace of guilt. They will forever languish in their *Status Quo*. There are current politicians that love politics and feel that their treacherous acts are somehow justified because they believe the people they are ruling over are more treacherous. Shakespeare's story of "All's Well That Ends Well," however, means that if the end result is good, then everything is good, but displaces the manipulative behavior that says that the ends justify the means. See the difference?

Selvedge

"Selvedge" is the edge of a woven fabric, which prevents the weave from becoming unraveled. It's completely different from the body of the fabric and it's an add-on to what is completely necessary so that the body of the fabric doesn't cease to exist and just become an unwoven mess.

Selvedge happens when resources are held in reserve so that an organization or family doesn't cease to exist. Some companies build selvedge with their margin. This margin is the profit on a transaction. The larger the margin, the larger area between the cost that is completely necessary to run a business and what is available to reinvest, hold as a resource, or use for a new venture so that the organization doesn't cease to exist in the future.

Selvedge happens in families mostly with time. When too much time is spent on the necessities of a family and no time is spent weaving selvedge and then something goes terribly wrong, a family will quickly unravel. We find that families that spend more selvedge-time together, even if that means cutting down on the necessities of life, have a harder time becoming unraveled. They stick together during those illnesses and financial hardships because they have a larger margin between what is absolutely necessary and what profits them as a family. In most families, LOVE is spelled TIME.

Selvedge also offers guidelines for an organization. It tells the organization where its limits are so the limits can be broadened. There was a study done on a schoolyard playground that was near a freeway. What we found was that the children that played on the playground were afraid of the freeway and huddled themselves close to the school building to keep themselves safe. That was until a fence was constructed around the schoolyard. Instead of the boundary fencing the children in, it offered freedom to venture out to the furthermost parts of the playground.

We could look at selvedge being a limitation or we could look at selvedge as being free so that we can explore the limits. I choose the latter.

Happiness Index

Pleasure is not a good indicator of what is good. If you simply look at my life and how money, although it provided pleasure to me, did not necessarily provide me what was good, you will see what emptiness was left after the money was gone. Ultimately what made me glad had little to do with money. Granted…money is a necessary part of this world, but too much emphasis is placed on acquiring it instead of treating it as a by-product of doing the right thing.

The following page charts out my gross income and what was going on in my life at that same time. I won't go into detail, but I made a lot of money in between 2002 and 2008. At that same time, though, the rest of my life was starting to unravel. My wife at the time knew, probably better than I did, that money should not be my source of joy. She told me early on that she was not happy and wanted to leave. I ignored her. I treated her as a commodity. She was the perfect trophy wife that I could take on trips across the nation or to different countries and she was classy and elegant.

I unwittingly put myself through a test and found out that if what I accomplished ruined the positive relationships in my life, those accomplishments were meaningless. I was intelligent enough not to be completely off track, so I chose to keep most of my relationships. But I attracted the wrong type of relationships and I avoided the right kind of relationships. I lost my wife of many years and the time I could spend with my children was cut in half. My heart ached so badly at times that I was sure that a heart attack was imminent. The pain that I felt was not worth the pleasure. There were moments where I would sit in a dark room where I languished. My arms felt like lead and I couldn't raise them to eyes that couldn't even produce the tears anymore. As the outside of me looked successful to the world, the inside of me was slowly dying. It seemed that I had everything that I needed, but pleasure is not a good indicator of what is good.

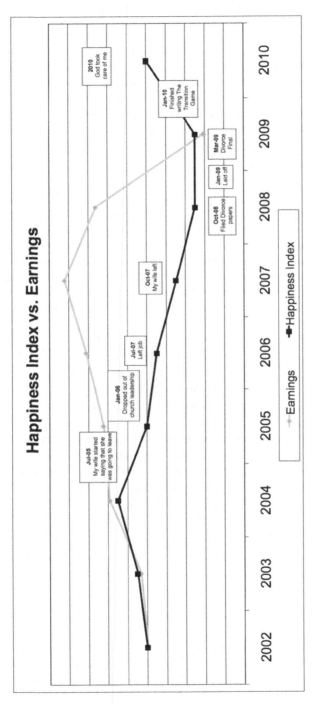

Happiness Index vs. Earnings

Jul-05 My wife started saying that she was going to leave

Jan-06 Dropped out of church leadership

Jul-07 Left job

Oct-07 My wife left

Oct-08 Filed Divorce papers

Jan-09 Laid off

Mar-09 Divorce Final

Jan-10 Finished writing The Transition Game

2010 God took care of me

◆ Earnings

■ Happiness Index

Lessons Learned

Your Commitment to Change is an endurance race not a sprint. You need a strong start and you need to reach your goals with vigor. You must build endurance for the long haul. It takes practice. Endurance and stamina have more to do with a balanced approach, though. They both take practice. We have hope because of the encouragement that endurance provides and we have more endurance because we are inspired by hope. The hope, encouragement, inspiration, and perseverance from endurance and stamina come from doing good.

To be Machiavellian means to be manipulative for dishonest gain and to be self-serving. Machiavelli was an "Ends Justifies the Means" mindset. You can put up with the not-so-fun-in-between-transitional times if you know the ending will be better, but that's different. Machiavellian people are sociopaths that have a grandiose view of themselves. They don't have the capacity to love so they lack the empathy to relate to the pain of others. They replace that lack of empathy with utter contempt for any kind of suffering. They can readily justify their crimes against other people without any trace of guilt. "All's Well That Ends Well," however, means that if the end result is good, then everything is good.

"Selvedge" is the edge of a woven fabric, which prevents the weave from becoming unraveled. Selvedge happens when resources are held in reserve so that an organization or family doesn't cease to exist. Some companies build selvedge with their margin. This margin is the profit on a transaction. Selvedge can also be built with time. We find that families that spend more selvedge-time together are more resistant to becoming unraveled. Selvedge also offers guidelines. It guides where its limits are so the limits can be broadened.

Pleasure is not a good indicator of what is good. Money is a necessary part of this world, but too much emphasis is placed on acquiring it instead of treating it as a by-product of doing the right thing. Money should not be a source of joy. If what we accomplish ruins the right relationships in our lives, those accomplishments are meaningless. The pain is not worth the pleasure. Pleasure is not a good indicator of what is good.

THE FIFTH C:
Commitment

Chapter 18
Execution

Execution

To execute is to produce as planned or designed. This means a plan or design was set in place so that you would know the end-result and, hopefully, move toward it. We commonly hear about executing judgment, but *Commitment to Change* is all about executing a plan. Executing a plan moves beyond judgment. A plan might proceed out of judgment, but judgment is limited. Without a plan, there would be no design and execution would not be arranged in any organized fashion. Rather, there would be no execution. The end-result may happen, but there is a slim chance that it will.

Execute with commitment. The use of daily (day to day) execution and a review of a long-term plan will produce the end-result that you desire. A plan that is seldom reviewed works against the planner. When a plan is devised and then put in the back of our minds without a daily or, at least, a weekly review, details become distorted and our direction that seems only a degree off in the beginning quite often misses the end-result by a wide margin. Daily or weekly reminders and refreshers cause slight corrections to be made and tweaks to be done so that wide fluctuations are not necessary.

When you're making corrections and tweaks along the way, do not second-guess your plan unless you're ready to discard it. To have confidence in the end-result means to stay the course AND to make course-adjustments. The word 'execute' comes from the Latin word execūtus, which is to follow up or carry out. You won't be able to carry out the plan if you're constantly questioning it. Beat the plan up and shoot holes through it as much as you can near the beginning, but there's a point that it just needs to be executed on. There will be time to go through iteration retrospectives after a plan turns into an on-going matter. If you remember…iteration retrospectives ask the questions, "What went well?," "What needs improvement?," and "What needs to be researched more?" If you ask and answer these questions well after each event, make adjustments, and then create patterns for better brain-muscle memories, then success is guaranteed.

Escape Velocity

In his 2011 book called "Escape Velocity"[10], Geoffrey Moore asks the question, "what if there is some hidden force that is working against your best efforts? And then he answers that question by defining hidden force as the pull of the past.

Essentially, you have to defy gravity to pursue the stars. Getting out of the *Status Quo* to your new *Commitment to Change* seldom happens by chance. There must be a way to do it. There must be a way to break free from the gravity that's holding your family, your organization, or yourself down.

But how do you escape the hold of the past? Why is it so easy to stay where you are? What lies have you been told that fool you into thinking that *Commitment to Change* is not important so that the *Status Quo* finally makes the torture slow and complete?

Think about the cost of living. Most people live from paycheck to paycheck. As their income grows, their expenses grow equally. People have talked themselves into thinking that they must get that better car. They must get that next relationship. They must have that next toy or they can't be truly happy. Many addictions are borne this way. People are constantly looking for their next best fix. A few people have figured out that in order to have nice things, they must save for them and not put something on interest that will cost them three times (in many cases much more) as much.

Something as simple as a savings account can provide escape velocity. Unfortunately, escape velocity won't happen without a cost. There are 3 costs to consider:

1. **The cost of hurting your pride** – It will hurt your pride to declare out loud that you've been doing something the wrong way. Set a goal and tell someone!

2. **The cost of ripping yourself away from benchmarking** – Benchmarks are good because they're a way to compare yourself

to the next guy and a way to tell if you're not totally out of bounds. But benchmarks hurt you because it's a way to compare yourself to the next guy and a way to tell if you're not totally out of bounds. Only rats run a rat race. If you're tired of being a rat, then you have to rip yourself away from benchmarking the rat race.

3. **The cost of time** – Time may be the biggest cost. Your time is worth something so you have to assess where you're going and if the time it takes to get there is worth the trip. Time must be taken in preparation and launch for a spacecraft in order for it to achieve the 7 miles per second that it takes to break away from the gravity of the earth. More time is spent preparing for the goal than actually achieving the goal.

Escape Velocity is the measurement of the rate and direction of your *Commitment to Change* in relation to your *Status Quo*. Unfortunately, what people don't realize about a poor *Status Quo* is that the cost to stay in that spot far exceeds the cost to achieve Escape Velocity.

39+1>40

During my time with Automatic Data Processing (ADP), our CEO, Josh Weston, would make annual visits and occasionally explain that 39 plus 1 is greater than 40 plus 0. There were always people in the crowd that didn't get it.

Before ADP became a prisoner to their own track record, there was a remedy for success. When I was with the company, we boasted 165 straight quarters of double digit earnings growth. That figure was bolstered by the idea of 39+1>40. In Josh Weston's words:

> *"Forty plus zero represents the busy person with a loaded in-basket while the phone is ringing every 15 seconds. In his 40-hour week, he's busy dealing with all of this stuff, with zero time to think about what he's doing and how he's doing it. A 39+1 person has the same in-basket and phone problem. Nevertheless, he will take one of his 40 hours to think about improving or eliminating some of what he's doing. A 39+1 person will get a lot more done than a 40+0 person."*

Josh was a great man and he ran his business well. You get more done by organizing first. I've seen people that have wanted to accomplish much, but have just spun their wheels in the mud because they can't get to everything at the same time. They don't plan and instead become that 40+1 person that just comes in and unproductively meanders through their job.

The Law of Unintended Consequences

Unintended Consequences are end-results that were not the original intention of a purposeful action. There are 3 types of unintended consequences:

- An unexpected benefit
- An unexpected drawback
- Perverse results

In a multi-faceted system that is so complex that it can't be defined, the law of unintended consequences warns against the belief that humans can fully control the world around them. As humans, we try to control our environment, but find that we don't take into account all of the factors. Now, people do need to make decisions and true *Commitment to Change* may not include all known factors. But since that's the case, there should be contingency planning put in place to plan for unintended consequences.

When I was in Aruba, we toured ships that were sunk during war time. These sunken ships created coral reefs, which are valuable to the sea life and, quite frankly, pretty to look at. This is an unexpected benefit from something horrific, which probably lost many lives.

Blowback is a term used by the CIA for the negative consequences to the civilian population by the aggressor government. You could say that Al Qaeda was the aggressor government in Iraq after the fall of Saddam Hussein. There was a pattern of contact between Hussein and Al Qaeda between 1990 and 1996, but Al Qaeda did not show power in that country until they started killing people in a terroristic fashion. Before that, Hussein could handle his own terroristic activity. The civilians that have been killed in Iraq by Al Qaeda since the fall of Hussein have experienced blowback.

In 2007, the New York Times reported on a case of perverse results[11]. Pongpat Chayaphan, acting Chief of the Crime Suppression Division in Bangkok, Thailand, said that officers were decorated with Hello Kitty armbands because "simple warnings no longer work" against police corruption (even the lowest level of corruption by parking in the wrong place, coming to work late, or dropping litter).

The original intention of this purposeful action was that it was "expected to make the officers feel guilt and shame and prevent them from repeating the offense, no matter how minor," he said. "Kitty is a cute icon for young girls. It's not something macho police officers want covering their biceps." Unfortunately, the officers started taking the armbands home as souvenirs, the idea failed, and police corruption increased.

It appears that there are *Commitments to Change* that are so dynamic that making broad sweeping changes while misunderstanding or without considering all the factors (or, at least, the most important ones) will not get you the desired result. That's why it's so important to base your changes on something proven and ask these following questions:

1. What has worked in the past?
2. Why has the desired result happened with that action that has worked in the past?
3. Am I looking at all the factors (or, at least, the most important ones)?
4. What contingency plan can I set in place to alter my actions in case of unintended consequences?

Live Within Your Means

If we live within our means, we will have a sustaining *Commitment to Change*. But living within your means must be a way of life. Change has to be a repeatable process in order for it to work over and over again. Seriously, life is so short that if you don't start right away, you won't get into the practice of living within your means. In the immortal words of Rod Stewart:

> *"Because life is so brief and time is a thief when you're undecided. And like a fistful of sand it can slip right through your hands."*

People search for options and sometimes that causes them to live outside of their means. Sometimes more options aren't any good. The risk is greater than the reward. Sadly, our society has defined "rich" in such a way that we must have the next best thing to be happy. These people misunderstand that they will be in slavery all their lives because of the fear of death. There is a deep yearning in each of them to get all they can now while they still have a chance because, to them, there is nothingness after death.

Instead, we all need to question our desires:

- Why do I desire what I desire?
- What changes once I get my desire?
- What costs and what benefits come from this desire?
- What is important?
- What part of my desires match up or conflict with my mission statement?

A good rule of thumb is to invest less than 30% of your income on shelter, save 10%, give 10% to a church or charity, and live on the rest.

Volunteerism

We commonly ask ourselves, "Is what I'm doing to help someone else actually making an impact?" This is a good question. But a common mistake is not committing to a charitable act because there might be the slightest risk that an impact will not be made or someone may misuse the charity. I am not saying that some type of risk assessment and cost/benefit analysis should not be made. Please do not misunderstand me. But when we don't have a desire to do something in the first place and the slightest risk gives us an excuse not to do anything, it becomes the wide and easy road to sit on our hands and not do what we know is right. Volunteer!

Don't ask, "How are you going to use this money?" to the person with a sign on the side of the road. I know this seems counter-intuitive, but if you have discerned that it is right to give to someone else, then give without red-tape. There are men and women that go into prisons where nobody else will go just to visit inmates and care for them. These men and women disregard their personal "feelings" and do what is right instead. This world is filled with people that want the inmates to be jailed and to simply rot. Unfortunately, most prisoners get out of jail at one time or another. The recidivism rate of ex-convicts follows the Pareto Principle. Sadly, it is normal for a cycle of 'crime-prison-reoffend-prison' to be repeated over and over again. The men and women that go into the prisons just to visit inmates and care for them actually fix core issues in some inmates' lives. Organizations like Kairos reverse the recidivism rate. They overturn the Pareto Principle and stop the negative cycle of ex-convicts reoffending and going back to prison. Along the same lines, many people complain about the high rate of illegal aliens crossing the border of Mexico, but they do nothing about the core issue. There are people that do the right thing and visit orphanages in Mexico to care for children and show them the better way of love. That fixes core issues. Too long we have covered wounds with bandages and not fixed underlying issues. After you have done your personal risk assessment and cost/benefit analysis and then have discerned what is right, find a way to volunteer in one way or another. Here are some ideas.

- Feed the hungry
- Give someone shelter
- Give clothes to the poor
- Visit people who are sick or in prison
- Help elderly widows
- Visit an orphanage
- Stand in the gap for someone else
- Give to the one who asks from you
- Don't turn away the one who wants to borrow from you

Lessons Learned

To execute is to produce as planned or designed. *Commitment to Change* is about executing a plan. Without a plan, there would be no design and execution would not be arranged in any organized fashion. Execute with commitment. A plan that is seldom reviewed works against the planner. Do not second-guess your plan unless you're ready to discard it. To have confidence in the end-result means to stay the course and to make course-adjustments. The word 'execute' comes from the Latin word executus, which is to follow up or carry out.

You have to defy gravity to pursue the stars. Getting out of the *Status Quo* to your new *Commitment to Change* seldom happens by chance. There must be a way to break free from the gravity that's holding you down. Escape velocity won't happen without a cost. It may be the cost of damaging your pride, the cost of ripping yourself away from benchmarking, or the simple cost of time. Escape Velocity is the measurement of the rate and direction of your *Commitment to Change* in relation to your *Status Quo*.

39 + 1 is greater than 40 + 0. A 39+1 person will get a lot more done than a 40+0 person. You get more done by organizing first. *Unintended Consequences* are end-results that were not the original intention of a purposeful action. There are 3 types of unintended consequences. They are

an unexpected benefit, an unexpected drawback, or a perverse result. The law of unintended consequences warns against the belief that humans can fully control the world around them. There should be contingency planning put in place to plan for unintended consequences.

Blowback is a term used for the negative consequences to the civilian population by the aggressor government. It's important to base your changes on something proven and ask these following questions: What has worked in the past? Why has the desired result happened with that action that has worked in the past? Am I looking at all the factors? What contingency plan can I set in place to alter my actions in case of unintended consequences?

If we live within our means, we will have a sustaining *Commitment to Change*. But living within your means must be a way of life. Change has to be a repeatable process in order for it to work over and over again. Sometimes more options aren't good. We all need to question our desires: Why do I desire what I desire? What changes once I get my desire? What costs and what benefits come from this desire? What is important? What part of my desire matches up or conflicts with my mission statement?

When we don't have a desire to do something in the first place and the slightest risk gives us an excuse not to do anything, it becomes far too easy to sit on our hands and not do what we know is right. If you have discerned that it is right to give to someone else, then give without hesitation. After you have done your personal risk assessment and cost/benefit analysis and then discerned what is right, find a way to volunteer in one way or another. Some ideas are listed in this chapter.

Chapter 19
Maintenance

Maintenance

Technically, there are different types of maintenance, but they all have this in common. All types of maintenance deal with care and upkeep. As you read the list below, think about how your *Commitment to Change* may be augmented by these different types of maintenance.

1. **Condition-Based Maintenance**
2. **Corrective Maintenance**
3. **Planned Maintenance**
4. **Predictive Maintenance**
5. **Preventive Maintenance**
6. **Proactive Maintenance**
7. **Reliability-Centered Maintenance**
8. **Value-Driven Maintenance**[12]

Condition-Based Maintenance happens when the need arises. In order for this type to be called maintenance, there must be condition monitoring. When an Early-Warning[2] arises, maintenance must be done.

Corrective Maintenance is intended to bring assets back within certain limits or tolerances after it has failed to remain within those boundaries.

Planned Maintenance is simply that...maintenance that is planned. Planned Maintenance is something that is scheduled ahead of time.

Predictive Maintenance takes experience. You know that when an asset runs, it will not run forever. There are certain breaking points that, with experience, you will see coming. This happens with humans as well as machines. Both are assets and both must be treated with care so that breaking points aren't met.

Preventive Maintenance consists of Condition-Based Maintenance and Planned Maintenance…specifically for the purpose of preventing major defects or down-time.

Proactive Maintenance focuses on root-causes and fixes core issues. Proactive Maintenance does not use bandage solutions that focus on symptoms.

Reliability-Centered Maintenance, or RCM, establishes minimum levels of maintenance to ensure that the asset continuously gets to the desired goal. This may require process improvements or tweaks to operating procedures.

Value-Driven Maintenance ensures future cash flows are secured. The *Status Quo* is not enough with Value Driven Maintenance (VDM). Long-Term thinking must be involved in this step. The 4 Value-Drivers are:

1. Utilizing the assets
2. Ensuring safety
3. Controlling costs
4. Allocating resources

No matter what the maintenance path you choose, they all involve care and upkeep. It's easier and more effective to maintain a healthy relationship or business than it is to repair a broken one. Heartache and pain come with shattered associations. If we can do what we can to maintain in one of the ways just listed, we will save ourselves anguish. Instead, we will be fruitful and productive. Everyone knows the saying, "an ounce of prevention is worth a pound of cure."

Lessons Learned

Simply, this chapter covered maintenance and the eight different types. The one commonality with Condition-Based, Corrective, Planned, Predictive, Preventive, Proactive, Reliability-Centered, and Value-Driven Maintenance is that they all involve care and upkeep. Maintenance can ensue when the need arises. Set up Early Warning Systems (EWS) to monitor conditions. If assets fail to remain within certain boundaries, corrections are needed. You can also schedule maintenance ahead of time. You don't want to have an asset reach its breaking point. It takes experience to predict when that breaking point might occur. You can prevent defects by scheduling maintenance when EWS signals a need. It will help any organization to use a pro-active approach with fixing problems instead of bandaging core issues. Establishing minimum levels of maintenance will ensure that assets get to desired goals. Long-Term thinking must be involved to utilize, ensure the safety of, control costs of, and allocate resources toward assets. It's easier and more effective to maintain a healthy relationship or business than it is to repair a broken one.

Chapter 20
Nehemiah Principle

The Nehemiah Principle

Think about the best way to lead your *Commitment to Change* and manage it like a project so you achieve the best of possible conclusions. How would you approach your commitment if your goal was to be effective? Consider the work of a well-known man named Nehemiah in a Middle-East building project. He employed the following steps to accomplish a task through exceptional Project Management and superior leadership skill.

- Vision
- Care
- Delegation
- Motivation
- Determination
- Conflict resolution
- Commitment to Change

These steps are commonly called The Nehemiah Principle and they can be used by anyone who wants to create a winning *Commitment to Change* and drive effectiveness in their lives. Let's investigate each step and understand how we can utilize them to consistently win.

Vision

Vision is where we intend to go with a project. This is a scary topic because nobody likes to fail and there is risk when we envision a goal, take steps toward that goal, and reach out to take hold of it. What if I'm wrong? What if this vision is misplaced and it's really just a fairy tale that I've talked myself into? I'm sure we've all met those dreamers that accomplish very little of anything. They just sit around all day and enter foolish controversies, talk about their genealogy, engage in arguments, and start quarrels. Those actions are unprofitable, useless, and lack vision. In order for vision to fit into the Nehemiah Principle, it must lead to effective action. You must see where you're going and seize the path.

Care

Nobody cares about what you know until they know how much you care. Most of you have heard that saying, but it's not just a cliché. That saying about how you should care has not lost its impact and the core meaning cannot be neglected. When a therapist practices client-centered care, there are three qualities that are essential:

1. Authenticity
2. Regard
3. Empathy

Care is what happens when we value something or someone and pay attention to it or them, respectively. Failure to care is just negligence. If you care enough about a project or person, you will make provisions and look out to ensure it grows. That takes attention and focus.

Delegation

A leader shouldn't do the job as well as the people do their job. If a leader isn't equipping and empowering the people that are following, that leader is not properly leading. Many people misunderstand "managing up." They might misconstrue "managing up" to "delegating up." Don't delegate up. Managing up includes helping with decisions, managing your boss's time, and turning data into useful information while delegating up just means giving your superiors work to do. Do the former not the latter.

Delegation is not dumping. It's not getting rid of accountability. And delegation is not just assigning work for the sake of assigning work. Delegation is assigning authority and responsibility to someone else to get the job done. You can't get rid of the accountability of the leader regardless of the amount of responsibility given. Delegation simply defines who does what by when based on ability, available resources, and timeframe.

Motivation

Avoidance of pain sells better than pursuit of pleasure. People will run away from pain faster than they run toward pleasure. Leaders know what causes pain and what produces pleasure and they help their people achieve the pleasure and avoid certain pain while achieving organizational goals at the same time. Done correctly, everyone on the team wins. Achieving all pleasure and avoiding all pain is not good so there must be some measure of altruism from the leader. Leaders are ineffective if they do not regard the welfare of others first. The key motivation for a leader must be anyone but themselves. Leaders have a duty and obligation to provide value to others. Stay away from the leaders that go into a situation with the sole purpose of some type of personal benefit.

The leader will uncover the reason to act in a certain way and this induces the action. In a nutshell, that is motivation. Motivate others and you can affect change in them so that they can do great things.

Determination

It's interesting how the word determination carries with it the absence of change and I put this word in a book called *Commitment to Change*. Determination has more to do with stability and constancy than it does with change itself. However, once the commitment has been made to change, determination is necessary for someone to stay the course and have singleness of purpose. In order for a person to realize a true *Commitment to Change*, they must be a staunch supporter of that change. Tommy Lasorda once said that the difference between the impossible and the possible lies in a person's determination.

Conflict Resolution

The only way to properly resolve conflict is to care enough to confront. In his book, "Caring Enough to Confront"[13], David Augsburger describes care-fronting. Humans by and large do not like conflict and when we shy away from conflict, it overpowers us. Confronting normally carries a negative connotation, but care-fronting says that you care about the relationship and the other person so much that you don't let conflict simmer and build.

Conflict resolution starts with understanding the motivation of the other person and helping them win. If we are critical of a person with whom we are having conflict, we must handle them constructively and not close ourselves off to the risk of being hurt by the other person. But the conflict must always be fair. As an example, even a boxer isn't supposed to hit below the belt.

Commitment to Change

The seventh and final stage of the Nehemiah Principle is what this book is all about, *Commitment to Change*. As you may remember *Commitment to Change* has five C's:

- **Consideration** – Evaluation of facts and careful thought
- **Certainty** – An assured fact
- **Charter** – An outline of conditions and organization with a definition of rights and privileges
- **Character** – The aggregate of features and traits that form the individual nature of a person with moral or ethical quality
- **Commitment** – The act of moving through The Transition Game with Consideration that brings Certainty and guidance from the Charter that brings Character

Move through *The Transition Game* with Consideration that brings Certainty and guidance from the Charter that brings Character. Do this well and your *Commitment to Change* will be sure!

The Nehemiah Principle uses leadership through vision, care, delegation, motivation, determination, and conflict resolution to obtain a "great" *Commitment to Change*. This principle helps you navigate through family and business waters so that you can win and help others win as well.

Lessons Learned

Lead your *Commitment to Change* and manage it like a project so it comes to the best of possible conclusions and approach it so that your goal is effective. Accomplish a task through exceptional Project Management and superior leadership skills with vision, care, delegation, motivation, determination, conflict resolution, and *Commitment to Change*. These steps, commonly called The Nehemiah Principle, can be used to create a winning *Commitment to Change*.

Vision is where we see we're going with a project. There is risk when we envision a goal, but you must see where you're going and seize the path. Three qualities are essential with care: authenticity, regard, and empathy. In these ways we value someone and pay attention to them. Failure to care is negligence. A leader shouldn't do a job all by themselves, nor are they able to do so. If a leader isn't equipping and empowering the people that are following him or her, that leader is not properly leading. Delegation is not dumping. It's not getting rid of accountability. Delegation simply defines who does what by when based on ability, available resources, and timeframe.

Avoidance of pain sells better than pursuit of pleasure. Leaders are ineffective if they do not regard the welfare of others first. The key motivation for a leader must be anyone but themselves. Leaders have a duty and obligation to provide value to others. Determination carries with it the absence of change. It has more to do with stability and constancy than it does with change itself. However, once the commitment has been made TO change, determination is necessary for someone to stay the course and have singleness of purpose. The only way to properly resolve conflict is to care enough to confront.

The seventh and final stage of The Nehemiah Principle is what this book is all about. *Commitment to Change* has five C's: Consideration, Certainty, Charter, Character, and Commitment. Commitment is the act of moving through *The Transition Game* with Consideration that brings Certainty and guidance from the Charter that brings Character.

Chapter 21
Learn from Failure

Learn from Failure

My dad would always say that you learn more from your failures than you do your successes. That is a true statement. The worst thing we can do for our children is to teach them that we do nothing wrong as parents. Rather, what we need to teach our children is that we fail and get back up to succeed. Succeeding, especially as parents, is important, but the first thing I taught my son and daughter when skiing was how to get up from a fallen position. The people that say, "I never fall down" don't even try. One of the main lessons you can teach your children is how to get up from a fall.

In my first book, *The Transition Game*, I wrote about 3 people: Benjamin Franklin, Thomas Edison, and Abraham Lincoln. These people we hold in high regard, but their lives were wrought with as much failure as success. Benjamin Franklin, who had many failures, was quoted as saying, "I didn't fail the test, I just found a hundred ways to do it wrong." Thomas Edison finally placed a carbonized thread into a vacuum sealed bulb to produce light after months of failing at his venture. He remarked, "Don't you realize that I have not failed, but have successfully discovered six thousand ways that won't work?" Abraham Lincoln was one of our greatest Presidents, but failed consistently from the 1830's through the 1850's before being elected President in 1860. Lincoln was defeated for state legislature, failed in business, had a nervous breakdown, was defeated for House Speaker, was defeated for nomination to Congress, was rejected for land officer, was defeated for U.S. Senate twice, and was defeated for nomination for Vice President. Of Course, when he was President, Lincoln was also able to draw on his prior successes during that same time. His successes included being elected company captain of the Illinois militia in the Black Hawk War, being appointed postmaster of New Salem, being appointed deputy surveyor of Sangamon County, being elected to Illinois state legislature multiple times, leading the Whig delegation in moving the Illinois state capital from Vandalia to Springfield, being nominated for Illinois House Speaker, being re-elected to the Illinois House, serving as Whig floor leader, establishing his own law practice, and being elected to Congress. By the time Abraham Lincoln was elected President of the United States of America, he had a wealth of experience (both failures and successes) that he was able to use to create great change.

Benjamin Franklin, Thomas Edison, and Abraham Lincoln all had this in common. They never became weary in doing good things. They absolutely knew they would reap the reward of their hard work as long as they didn't lose heart in the process…and they knew how to get back up.

Playing from Behind

Once you've fallen behind, it's hard to get back in front. Whether it's sports, grades, class-work, your job, and especially marriage. It's difficult, at best, to play catch-up. Yes, it would be easier to just start out ahead, but let's get real. Falling behind often happens and playing from behind has become the norm. When I played any kind of sports, I hated playing from behind because I found myself becoming one-dimensional. There was a sense of urgency trying to draw even with someone else. I didn't play my own game and my stress level increased. I'm a competitive guy, but my wish to attain the same progress as another person (brought on by my competitiveness) hurt me. I couldn't get out ahead and then manage my game.

Before my divorce, I was even competitive with my wife, Michelle. And let me just say that competitiveness between a husband and wife is not good. You'll find a worthy adversary across the dinner table. If you go in that direction, you'll find out. Well, I blindly went in that direction and I quickly fell behind. There were no winners in our divorce. Neither one of us got what we wanted. We hurt ourselves and our children suffered emotionally and will probably be affected for the rest of their lives. I'm truly sorry for how I handled things. I was foolish. I looked to be at least equal with Michelle in every aspect of our life when, plainly, she was better at some life-pieces than I was.

Playing from behind is not a remedy for success. Conversely, starting strong allows a favorable environment to exist so you can seek further favorable conditions where success will build on itself. The pact that my friend,

Pat Roy, and I made to raise strong 30-year olds meant that we would start strong to guide our children practically, emotionally, and spiritually so that they would grow up to be functioning and strong adults. Starting out strong works. Playing from behind does not.

Ugly but Effective

I used to have a saying with my son's baseball teams when they would make a completely unorthodox, but great play. "Ugly but Effective." It seemed during these plays that the player's goal was to make the play without a care about how their body looked doing it. I would rather be ugly but effective if I had to make the choice between the two.

If you look at Tim Tebow, you'll see something similar in his professional and personal life. You'll see someone who consistently wins. He doesn't really care about how he looks and what might cause disapproval with his critics. I noticed this with the way he plays football and the way he shares his faith. The only reason that he seeks to perfect his motion is to consistently make plays. He repeatedly practices the right motion so that he can perfect it. He doesn't just reiterate his faith to vainly repeat what he's saying. There is genuineness with Tim Tebow that makes him effectively fervent. I chose the word fervent because that word shows great warmth. There is an intensity of spirit and he shows immense enthusiasm that anyone watching would say is burning. His spirit glows with that white-hot heat.

That intensity, enthusiasm, and white-hot heat inspire people. When Tim was a Denver Bronco, the fan base was clamoring for him to start as quarterback because he generated a spark. He instilled that confidence that they would win...and they did win. He also instilled that confidence in his teammates. You would hear the occasional comment from people wishing he would just shut up, but his teammates did respect him. Plainly, there is something about this guy that causes a stir in a polarizing fashion. How can someone be chosen as a starter over another quarterback with better numbers? How can a quarterback start after completing two passes against the Chiefs? Tim Tebow is a starter because he won that particular game against the Chiefs in which he only completed two passes.

Interestingly, the players from other teams that have mocked him were themselves disgraced that very same season. Simply, Tim doesn't think it's all about him. He gives glory to his God. The players that mock Tim Tebow won't have a thing to worry about with any retaliation from Tim. Their problems are much bigger.

Tim has found out what winning is like by the effective, albeit unconventional, use of his skills. It may not be pretty, but it sure is successful.

Acidophilus

Commitment to Change is like acidophilus. Acidophilus is one of those "good bacteria" that help a human body. It normally can be found raw or in yogurt or fermented soy products. The Latin words lactobacillus acidophilus literally means "acid-loving milk-bacterium." I'm not a doctor, but some of the touted health benefits range from reducing diarrhea to preventing cancer. People who drink it vary from those who are lactose-intolerant to people going through chemotherapy. Of course, over-dosage of anything is dangerous so prudence is important…but still, Acidophilus can improve your digestive system and immune system.

There is also a side effect called the Jarisch-Herxheimer reaction, which causes the skin of people with a current condition who are taking acidophilus to have their skin actually worsen before it gets better. Many of these people felt sick and feverish. Initially, their skin became more blemished. This is how Acidophilus is like your *Commitment to Change*. In the right dosage a great *Commitment to Change* can purify your business process, relationships, and your peace of mind. Expect that it may cause blemishes to come to the surface. You may have to deal with the unexpected results of your *Commitment to Change* because the right process uncovers toxins under the surface.

When blemishes come to the surface, the worst thing that can happen is to cover them with make-up. A cover-up seals the impurities in place and sinks into the surface with its own poison. The *Commitment to Change*, struggling to purify the structure, loses its power to push the bad processes and habits out of the system. If a great *Commitment to Change* is allowed to act as intended with no cover-up of bad processes or habits, it will push those toxins out of the system, bring them to the surface, and, as long as there is a good cleaning, the clean underneath will be revealed. After Acidophilus and a great *Commitment to Change* are complete, what is underneath is now healthy, vibrant, and free from disease.

Lessons Learned

We learn more from our failures than we do our successes. We may fail, but we must get back up to succeed. The people that we hold in high regard have lives that were wrought with as much failure as there were successes. Out of these failures and successes came experiences that they were able to use to create great change. They never became weary in doing good things. They absolutely knew they would reap the reward of their hard work as long as they didn't lose heart in the process…and they knew how to get back up.

It's easier to start out ahead, but falling behind often happens. When this happens, a sense of urgency ensues and we may not play our own game. It's better to manage the game. Playing from behind is not a remedy for success. Conversely, starting strong allows a favorable environment to exist where you can seek further favorable conditions where success will build on itself.

It's okay to make the play without caring about how we look doing it. I would rather be ugly but effective if there had to be a choice between the two. Still, we should seek to perfect our motion to consistently make plays. Repeatedly practicing the right motion can perfect that motion, but there must be genuineness to be effectively fervent. Being fervent has an intensity of spirit and immense enthusiasm. It instills confidence. Winning comes about by the effective, albeit unconventional, use of our skills.

Commitment to Change may cause blemishes to come to the surface. You may have to deal with the unexpected results because the right process uncovers toxins under the surface. A cover-up seals the impurities in place and sinks into the surface with its own poison. The *Commitment to Change*, struggling to purify the structure, loses its power to push the bad processes and habits out of the system. If a great *Commitment to Change* is allowed to act as intended with no cover-up of bad processes or habits, it will push those toxins out of the system, bring them to the surface, and, as long as there is a thorough cleaning, the clean surface will reveal the clean underneath.

Commitment
CASE STUDY

Commitment Case Study

Chapter 22
Commitment to Change
A Case Study

Jim is just a regular guy. He learned how to work hard from his parents and he has a wife that loves him. He loves her in return and loves his children as well. I was looking at some pictures that his wife, Janette, had taken of Jim and one of them had the caption, "what a man!" He knows that he may have been too strict with his children, but that it's because he loves them. He has a work ethic that you seldom see and he is a great friend.

James Richard Schueller II was born with a health condition...something that takes away mortal life and suffocates a human body. He has ALS "Lou Gehrig's Disease." Formally, Amyotrophic Lateral Sclerosis, which literally means not having muscle nourishment. It leads to a scarring of the nerve cells as it degenerates. Jim explained that he will probably choke on his food and eventually that would be what kills him. He doesn't want medical heroics. His hero is Jesus Christ.

Jim did better than the doctors had predicted. Within a few months of being diagnosed, they said his muscles would atrophy to such a point that he would be unable to walk and perform basic functions. I remember the morning well almost two years later when a few of us got the message that Jim wouldn't be joining us for breakfast as we had all planned. He just couldn't get up. Janette went and bought a wheelchair that day...she watched her man start to fade away and could do nothing about it.

I talked to Jim and Janette the following week and told them that I threw away what I had written in this chapter because it was unfocused. I wasn't capturing Jim's and his family's *Commitment to Change*. I asked each of them what their commitment was. Jim answered immediately...that his commitment was to love and to show love, but when I turned to Janette and she responded, I received an answer that I wasn't expecting. "To stay… because I don't know if I can handle this," she said. I was looking at the strongest woman that I had ever known in this world and I was stunned by the truth she had spoken. I don't consider Janette strong because of her physical abilities because she is petite. But she has a character that I have not seen elsewhere.

Jim had seen plenty of death, but Janette hadn't experienced it at all and now it was hitting home…in her home. With the man she had connected with at the deepest level…with her man. You can tell by the way she looks at him, that this is a love story that most of us dream about. Sure, distractions come across our path and we become angry with our mate, but Jim and Janette experienced that deep love that not many people know. When they started dating in high school, they both felt like they were "dating up." Jim was more than complimentary of Janette and she was flattered that this very attractive popular guy would be interested in her.

My son, Nathan, said that when he thinks of Jim, he thinks of his faith. Jim has a great faith. He never questioned what happens after he dies. When people would tell me that "everyone questions what will happen after they die," I would point them to a man I know that has the faith of a mustard seed. He could move big mountain-sized problems.

Jim's purpose statement is that he "lives to serve by loving his fellow brothers and sisters that are In Christ and not In Christ…and ministering to others"

I want to talk about Jim's family as much as about him and what they did to keep their *Commitment to Change.* You see, Jim's commitment was easier for him. I know that seems cold and callous for me to say, but I can say it because Jim is a true friend and his faith was never questioned. He had maintained his life to such a point that it was easier for him to transition through the 5 C's. There wasn't much to consider before he was certain about what needed to happen. Immediately, he began his charter by making decisions while he could still take care of his family. His character was beyond reproach and he had already made the commitment when he was young. Now, he just needed to finish his life strong. His commitment was short term not because of his decision about how to live, but rather about how to die.

I'm finding it hard to continue writing as Jim and I talk together. This book is written through eyes that are clouded by tears. I wish I could have faith like Jim. That I would experience a *Commitment to Change* so real that it goes to the very fiber of my being. My commitments pale in comparison to his. God made a mighty man. Before I hung up the phone after I talked with him I would tell him that I love him and he would say the same...and it never seemed odd for one grown man to tell another one that they loved each other.

Jim might not know what change is being accomplished by the people that will read his story. I'm like Jim because it's more important that the message has been communicated so that an accomplishment can be obtainable by whoever reads his story. It's up to the reader to decide if they want to live a fulfilled life that means something or be self-centered in that what their life produces doesn't amount to much. I don't know if God will tell Jim how many lives he affected, but I do know he's headed for an eternal life that is so much better than this one.

I want to differentiate between what I call legacy-thinking and Jim's desire to leave a legacy for his children. Legacy-thinking often times has an incorrect or incomplete construction, but Jim's legacy will be that he finished his life better than he began because he fought the good fight.

When Jim found out about his illness, he immediately brought his close friends around him to pray and lay hands on him. I was fortunate to be included in his circle. He realized that he had a short time and that his life commitment would be somewhat unrealized unless it was defined and communicated. He had already reverse-engineered his life, studied it, and was transformed by the renewing of his mind, but he hadn't communicated that to anyone. The communication piece was the difficult part for Jim.

Jim's life is strong and vibrant because he approached a commitment to his faith with consideration that brought certainty through character from his charter. He's one of the fortunate ones that can look back at his life with absolute assurance that he did well despite his shortcomings.

I wrote this case study, deleted it, and re-wrote it with Janette's and Jim's help because it seemed unfocused. I desired to tell too much of Jim's life and the study was distracted by the details. Suddenly, I realized that

I needed to understand what caused Janette's and Jim's life to become a self-sustaining chain reaction that will continue with their children.

Early on in Jim's life, his output was based on the capacity of his constraint that he used as a child, his medicine. He simply identified certain medicines as a constraint, studied them through focus, and then elevated himself past them and was then free from his bonds to those drugs.

I spoke to Janette and Jim about doing what was necessary AND sufficient in Jim's final days. In this way, their vision was assured. Jim was steadfast with what he wanted to communicate. He spent a lot of time with people and didn't seclude himself at the end of his mortal days. He communicated with care to his children and he stood ready to meet his maker. He knew his roles as husband, father, and friend and conducted himself in a manner worthy of those positions. This disease didn't win over Jim. Jim won over the disease. He lived a life that transcends mortality and had a heart for his God that few understand.

Jim had that "long time" perspective and he was successful because of it. He goes to his death as a willing participant because the greatness that he desires is to be with the Almighty. He realized that discounting the short-term was not good so he spent extra time with those he loved. A lot of people love Jim and Janette. They stand on their own, but they stand together. One person on the team will be brought to the Lord and one will be here to carry on until that day comes for her too. Janette's job may be harder, but friends will gather around her and care for her. When she calls, able men will stand ready to care for her family. Janette never had to deal with death until this happened to Jim and she was not prepared for this to happen so soon.

Jim, nevertheless, encouraged the people around him despite the pain he was enduring. His mother called this process "hell," but this is the worst that he would endure…while this life is the best that some would endure. Sean Oliver, my executive coach, filmed Jim's final messages and that will be made available so that they can see Jim's encouragement. Jim propped us up on his weakened shoulders. He told us the hard bitter truth to strengthen us for a better day. He provides hope. He shared his knowledge and imparted his wisdom without asking us to take his word for it.

Jim was fully convinced and I'll seek to imitate him as he obtains his dream through his faith and patience. Still, and I won't downplay Jim's illness, it's easier to be fully convinced when the path is as clear as Jim's was. There was so much uncertainty with the rest of the family and what this life was bringing next that it was much harder to lock themselves in. They did prove that they were all in, but many of us waited holding our breath as we saw Jim's and Janette's goals were actually the same.

Jim had a unique way of using emotions in the proper context and with the right motivation. He always had a light spirit unless he was correcting someone, but those corrections occurred less and less as his days shortened. This Emotional Intelligence that Jim personified allowed him to make good decisions. Still, unilateral decisions, which probably wouldn't have been optimum were made because Jim felt like he knew best and didn't have time to consult with his family. Jim knew that he didn't deserve to be happy because the joy he experienced in his heart despite the disease wasn't from him. He chose to use the right emotion and generate feelings so that he was not controlled by what was happening around and inside him.

I can't explain Jim's optimism because I don't entirely understand it. He searched for different options to treat ALS, but then didn't worry about it. He knew we could not add a single hour to our lives by worrying and his choices reflected that. He had many things to think about, but nothing to worry about. He approached his problem with quality and character. He was awake and alert as much as he could be. Jim was controlled with humbleness by his conscience according to how God wanted him to be.

Jim may have been humble, but he realized his value. He didn't undervalue himself. His pain was useful because his remedy was a testimony for others. Jim never needed to feel validated because his value came from his God. His God already made him valid. His life was worth something. He gauged his results by seeing his children thrive. I was fortunate enough to see his daughter sing at a rodeo that was given just for Jim. Jim set his own sights on getting his message across. He investigated, searched, examined, and inquired to have his own vision and then used his own voice to announce his Commitment to Change. He used every sense available to him while he could. He, ultimately, detached himself from his mortal outcome.

Jim used a blueprint as an outline for his plan of action. He brought together friends so that he could bounce ideas off of them and then adjusted accordingly. He attempted to remove, go around, or go through this ALS barrier, but there was not a whole lot of contingency planning except for his prayer life.

He did his best to bring everyone on the same page to his illness, but he cared for his wife so much that he dreaded to tell her when it first happened. Pain and heartache gripped him for her and he avoided her phone calls after he first heard because he couldn't bear to tell her. He didn't know how she would handle it. He misunderstood that her perfect dissimilarities would complement and leverage the understanding of interdependence. Nevertheless, Janette and Jim were aligned to the purpose and mission of their lives. They investigated the rules and sought multiple reference points. They looked at this disease from different vantage points and, thus, provided a true picture of their *Commitment to Change.*

Janette found it difficult to handle her emotions so that she could carry on. Her mind had all the knowledge of all those comfort verses and promises running throughout God's word. She constantly was before God. She conversed with Him about giving every worry, sadness, and negative thought to Him, but her body battled against her just as Jim's body battled against him. Their minds had complete knowledge of God's grace and will, but their bodies were not as cooperative. Control is an illusion of youth. Janette became disillusioned with every year she got older. Jim's illness just accelerated things. The only thing we can control is our thinking and our responses to situations. This really put life into perspective. God is all that mattered to her and she still had her responsibilities. She knew that if she really couldn't control anything, then the only thing she had to ground herself is following the lead of someone who does.

Teamwork meant that Janette and Jim had different functions in one common goal. Janette submitted herself to Jim's purpose while he was still around. This was a difficult task and she made herself physically sick over getting Jim's purpose right while losing the man she loved. Janette knows that she can't do this life all by herself. It's not "needy" to need other people. We weren't designed to go it alone. She will have women and men that will add value to her life, recognize common issues, discover new resources for her children, and create sustainability in her life after Jim leaves this earth.

Jim was always good at observing his surroundings. What made him such a strong foreman at his job was that after he observed the environment around him, he would quickly orient himself to see what needed to happen so he would have decisive action. He gained an advantage at work and in sports this way. He created patterns that worked. Those same patterns were used with his family, but didn't always work as well. He started to realize just in time how important the other person was in the relationship…what his family meant to him…and how much he wanted to show his love. Few of us get this chance to see what we need to do before we die because our death comes slowly and isn't immediate. This life normally lulls us into this false sense of complacency and we relax our efforts to reach out to others. Jim didn't have that luxury. His life would be ending shortly and he had little time to ask "how could he do it better?"

As Jim ventured out into each new action, he stayed connected to his God so he could be productive and effective. He admitted that he would be unable to do anything without Him and gladly Jim would say that he was okay with his life being plastered all over the newspaper tomorrow. Jim didn't fool himself by saying "I have the right!" and seek after his own desires. Instead, he sought what was good and right. Sure, Jim seldom went at a project or event without a plan where he could obtain a specific goal or result, but to him the ends never justified the means. Doing it the right way was just as important to Jim as doing the right thing. He never made his Plan B his plan A. He never wound up having the chance. He was intentional and deliberate about his success.

Jim was the genuine article. He cared deeply for others and inspired confidence. He was transparent and let his light shine on every situation.

As he crafted his final message, he was open and accountable and allowed others to give him input. He gathered people around him that would raise his level so he wouldn't stagnate. In the end, he simplified his message so others could understand it better and he communicated well before and after the disease muddled his speech.

Jim and Janette's loving and caring for each other didn't come with a parade. They were characterized by this love and care. People saw it from the outside. Their hearts were right, good, and pure. I'm not saying that they did nothing wrong. They both are human after all. Did they act in the most appropriate way at all times?…Of course not. But they showed the kind of love that only few dream about. There were not a lot of words and fanfare. It wasn't their practice to make empty promises. They concerned themselves with greater things.

To Janette, 'Till Death Do Us Part' meant just that. She encouraged Jim by letting him know that she wasn't going anywhere. She was there until 'death

COMMITMENT TO CHANGE **149**

do us part'. That gave Jim assurance during his mortal life. She is a woman of integrity because she considered her husband's thoughts, feelings, and desires with every decision she made. She made every attempt to make him feel important and respected. Jim knew that life was much better with Janette in it. She made his life complete. Outsiders to their relationship saw their relationship as a true love-affair.

Jim subordinated himself to a higher purpose. He is, at the time I'm writing this book, mature and productive. He is just, equitable, and true, which allowed his actions to be grounded with reason that determined his conduct. He pursued justice, sought kindness and mercy, and walked humbly. He was peacefully innocent, but not naïve. Jim was astute and sharp.

Now, Janette needs to endure and reach her goals with vigor and stamina. Her purpose is to show Christ's love. She has an endurance race, but she will persevere because she has the same mighty God that Jim has. She has hope because of the encouragement that endurance provides and she has more endurance because she is inspired by that hope. Janette will build enough selvedge so that it will prevent her family from becoming unraveled. She will execute with commitment and she won't second-guess her plan. She will live within her means and she will have a sustaining *Commitment to Change*. She will ask those hard questions: Why do I desire what I desire? What changes once I get my desire? What costs and what benefits come from this desire? What is important? What part of my desire matches up or conflicts with my mission?

Jim handled his disease in a matter-of-fact manner so his worldly end came to the best possible conclusion. He learned how to love his wife all over again. That love will be carried into his eternal life. They showed authenticity, regard, and empathy toward each other and they valued one another because they paid attention. Jim couldn't avoid this pain, but he learns his final lessons because this pain and Janette's pain can't be avoided. They stayed the course together and had a singleness of purpose. Her children know that she will love them no matter what and she will teach them the skills they need to grow to be spiritually, mentally, emotionally, and physically balanced people. Janette explains why she is telling them to do something. She teaches her children how she thinks and not just what she thinks. She has certainty that God will provide for her family. She's been assured because of the constant provisions that she has seen in the past.

Jim and Janette love and respect each other because they know they must and are controlled by Christ. They never became weary in doing good things for each other. They absolutely knew that they would reap the reward of their hard work in due season as long as they didn't lose heart in the process...and they knew how to get back up together...even when they physically couldn't.

They exemplified *Commitment to Change*...the commitment that moved through transition with Consideration that brings Certainty and guidance from their Charter that brought Character.

James Richard Schueller II
November 4, 1973 – February 18, 2013
Survived by his wife Janette
Children – Sierra, Skylar, and Slater
Parents – Jim & Liana
Sisters – Erina and Tina
Nieces and Nephews

"Yet those who wait for the Lord Will gain new strength;
They will mount up with wings like eagles,
They will run and not get tired,
They will walk and not become weary."
Isaiah 40:31

Notes

[1] "The Unheavenly City; The Nature and Future of our Urban Crisis" by Edward C. Banfield, 1970, Little, Brown

[2] "The Transition Game" by Greg Olney, 2010, Createspace.com Publishing

[3] "About Teepa Snow" www.teepasnow.com, © Teepa Snow [teepasnow.com] Occupational Therapist and Consultant

[4] "Development Milestones" The University of Michigan Health System, Written and compiled by Kyla Boyse, R.N. Reviewed by Layla Mohammed, M.D., Updated February 2010

[5] The Jethro Principle – Harvard Business Review from Exodus 18

[6] "Good to Great" by Jim Collins, 2001, Harper Business

[7] "How the mighty fall: and why some companies never give in" by James Charles Collins, Collins Business 2009

[8] "Principle-Centered Leadership" by Stephen R. Covey, Simon & Schuster, 1990, 1991

[9] "The Art of War" by Sun Tzu, 544-496 B.C.

[10] "Escape Velocity: Free Your Company's Future from the Pull of the Past" by Geoffrey A. Moore, HarperCollins Publishers 2011

[11] "To Punish Thai Police, a Hello Kitty Armband" by Seth Mydans, New York Times August 7, 2007

[12] "Maintenance" Wikipedia: http://en.wikipedia.org/wiki/Maintenance

[13] "Caring Enough to Confront" by David Augsburger, 1986, Regal Books

[14] "No Substitute for Victory: Lessons in Strategy and Leadership from General Douglas MacArthur" by Theodore Kinni and Donna Kinni

Index

Martin Vogel *by Tara Thiesmeyer*

Photo by Martin Vogel

Martin Vogel has a talent for invention... and for reinvention. His life so far has included several successful careers in vastly different fields, and his potential for more is unlimited. In fact, limitation in any form is an unknown concept to Vogel. He likes a challenge, and he puts his heart and soul into everything he does.

His first career was racing motorcycles. He jumped into that sport at the tender age of 5, started road racing at 16, and at 20 was a professional on the American Motorcycle Association Formula 2 circuit. A natural competitor, Vogel was racing grand prix events at tracks such as Laguna Seca and Daytona, Florida.

In the midst of his racing success, everything changed. He was warming up on the Infinion Raceway in Sonoma, California, when another cyclist collided with Vogel and sent him flying into the hay bales... then his own bike hit him and broke his back. With a T3 spinal cord injury, he was paralyzed from the chest down. Was his life over at the age of 21? Absolutely not! Vogel is a champion, and that hadn't changed.

The usual recovery time for injuries that severe is six or seven months, but Vogel wheeled out of rehabilitation in only seven weeks, with a drive to conquer this new challenge. He also had a new inspiration, another paraplegic had shown him that he could continue racing but in his wheelchair. He encouraged Vogel to enter the Los Angeles Marathon. At first Vogel was skeptical about taking on such a demanding, physical feat only a couple months out of rehab, with all the adjustments he had to make to his new form of mobility. But, with his friend's coaching he finished the race.

Vogel has since won countless races of various distances in his wheelchair, including the Long Beach Marathon in October 2012. He gained sponsorship from McDonald's and toured Europe and North America competing. He is a seven-time world champion in the 5000 meter. He not only made a living for many years racing in his chair, he encouraged other wheelchair athletes as well. He trains as seriously as any other professional, and he is an advocate for the sport to be more widely accepted and promoted. He has custom adapted or invented many of the features of his racing chair, race gear, and specialized equipment and shared his creations with others.

He also races super karts (and can be seen on YouTube in them), having designed hand controls to drive the kart. His real victory there, however, is in coaching young competitors in the sport. Kids are Vogel's favorite companions, and he loves teaching them life lessons while sharing his understanding of how to be a champion.

Racing is not Vogel's only passion. At the same time he was first learning how to ride a bike, he also discovered a love for creating art. From childhood he has enjoyed illustration, pottery, welding sculpture, watercolor, and painting in acrylic. His high school art teacher was a special mentor to him, and after his accident she helped him channel his emotions and boundless energy into an art career. He continued his exploration through college classes and private study, especially in the mastery of color.

Then one day he was going up a trail with some friends, and when he turned around to wait for them to catch up, he noticed all the tracks he had made in the dirt. Recognizing the potential for a new method of painting, he started practicing down at the park making patterns on the ground with his wheelchair. He then rigged up an old chair with devices to apply paint to the wheels, which could then be transferred directly onto a canvas. Thus began his invention of wheelchair painting, which has since inspired other artists.

Vogel paints elaborate patterns with his wheelchair, sometimes in beautiful symmetry, other times with more wild abandon. His subjects are usually abstract, but he has also outlined elegant nudes, using only his wheels. Then, he paints between the lines in eye-catching color combinations, creating canvases rich in visual harmony. His works range in size from 1' x 1' to 6' x 7' to massive 4' x 22' creations. He has also done series of three and six panels in a row. The finished painting might be dark and elaborate, with painstaking detail in the process, or it could be bright, graphic, and fun.

To date he has completed over 800 canvases, as well as hundreds of works in other

Photo by Tara Thiesmeyer

media. He has painted large commissions for hotels, offices, and restaurants. He has held exhibitions all over California as well as in Washington, D.C. and Texas. He has appeared in numerous magazines, newspapers, and television programs. He got more high-profile exposure when he was invited to paint the Olympic rings in front of the President of the I.O.C., and another one of his pictures was made into a poster for the 2002 Winter Olympics in Salt Lake City.

Martin painting "Spiritual Twins," featured on the cover, on the sidewalk in front of his Pasadena, CA studio

Vogel also has a dream of bringing more art outlets to children. He often demonstrates his techniques at school assemblies, and he loves teaching kids to explore their own artistic potential. He hopes to raise money for public school programs and to continue to be a mentor to young people to believe in their own futures.

Anyone who encounters Martin Vogel is invariably impressed with his artwork, inspired by his story, and intrigued by his personality. What he invents next, with his artwork and his life, we can't wait to see.

(626) 673-1800 • artinvoge@sbcglobal.net • www.martinvogel.com